THE COMPLETE IDIOT'S GUIDE® TO

Fondues and Hot Dips

by Ellen Brown

ALPHA

A member of Penguin Group (USA) Inc.

Fondue is about sharing, so this book is dedicated to Kim Montour,
the best friend a person could have, with whom I've shared so much.

ALPHA BOOKS

Published by the Penguin Group

Penguin Group (USA) Inc., 375 Hudson Street, New York, New York 10014, USA

Penguin Group (Canada), 10 Alcorn Avenue, Toronto, Ontario, Canada M4V 3B2 (a division of Pearson Penguin Canada Inc.)

Penguin Books Ltd, 80 Strand, London WC2R 0RL, England

Penguin Ireland, 25 St Stephen's Green, Dublin 2, Ireland (a division of Penguin Books Ltd)

Penguin Group (Australia), 250 Camberwell Road, Camberwell, Victoria 3124, Australia (a division of Pearson Australia Group Pty Ltd)

Penguin Books India Pvt Ltd, 11 Community Centre, Panchsheel Park, New Delhi—10 017, India

Penguin Group (NZ), cnr Airborne and Rosedale Roads, Albany, Auckland 1310, New Zealand (a division of Pearson New Zealand Ltd)

Penguin Books (South Africa) (Pty) Ltd, 24 Sturdee Avenue, Rosebank, Johannesburg 2196, South Africa

Penguin Books Ltd, Registered Offices: 80 Strand, London WC2R 0RL, England

Copyright © 2006 by Ellen Brown

International Standard Book Number: 1-579257-576-5
Library of Congress Catalog Card Number: 2006927532

08   07   06   8   7   6   5   4   3   2   1

Interpretation of the printing code: The rightmost number of the first series of numbers is the year of the book's printing; the rightmost number of the second series of numbers is the number of the book's printing. For example, a printing code of 06-1 shows that the first printing occurred in 2006.

Printed in the United States of America

Note: This publication contains the opinions and ideas of its author. It is intended to provide helpful and informative material on the subject matter covered. It is sold with the understanding that the author and publisher are not engaged in rendering professional services in the book. If the reader requires personal assistance or advice, a competent professional should be consulted.

The author and publisher specifically disclaim any responsibility for any liability, loss, or risk, personal or otherwise, which is incurred as a consequence, directly or indirectly, of the use and application of any of the contents of this book.

Most Alpha books are available at special quantity discounts for bulk purchases for sales promotions, premiums, fund-raising, or educational use. Special books, or book excerpts, can also be created to fit specific needs.

For details, write: Special Markets, Alpha Books, 375 Hudson Street, New York, NY 10014.

Publisher: *Marie Butler-Knight*
Editorial Director: *Mike Sanders*
Managing Editor: *Billy Fields*
Acquisitions Editor: *Michele Wells*
Senior Development Editor: *Christy Wagner*
Production Editor: *Megan Douglass*

Copy Editor: *Emily Garner*
Cover Designer: *Bill Thomas*
Book Designers: *Trina Wurst/Kurt Owens*
Indexer: *Julie Bess*
Layout: *Chad Dressler*
Proofreader: *Mary Hunt*

Contents at a Glance

Contents

What the recipe symbols mean:

▲ Fast

● Healthy

■ Make-ahead

✚ Vegan

Introduction

Fondue is fast food that's meant to be eaten at a leisurely pace with friends and family gathered around the table. That's a great part of its renewed popularity. Eating fondue is about enjoying time at the table in a relaxed way and reveling in the experience of eating. It's about savoring. It's about talking while dipping and dunking. It's about sharing time and sharing thoughts.

This relaxation starts with the person who prepared the fondue. Guests at a fondue fête feed themselves and, in the case of oil and broth fondues, actually cook the food themselves.

While fondue parties with guests are festive, the recipes in this book shouldn't be relegated to infrequent evenings when entertaining. They're meant for everyday eating, too. Many studies have highlighted that in today's world, family members tend to eat at different times due to the demands of schedules. Making a fondue pot the centerpiece of a family dinner table brings everyone back home. In probably less time than it takes to create the average family meal, you've created a family dining occasion, an opportunity for your family to truly listen to one another. Plus, dipping a new vegetable into a fondue is a pleasurable way to expand your children's culinary horizons.

Fondue may have passed from popularity for the past 30 years, but the same cannot be said for dips of all temperatures, including the hot ones in this book. Few people make dips for a family meal, but I bet you can't think of a party you've attended that didn't have at least one dip.

Dips are easy on hosts. There's no last-minute assembly of hors d'oeuvres, and there's no need to pass anything during the party. After the party is over, there's no mountain of small plates stacked up like the Leaning Tower of Pisa awaiting washing in the kitchen.

And dips are easy on guests. They can eat dips with one hand so there's no need for a juggling lesson to learn how to simultaneously handle glasses, forks, and plates. Dips encourage people to talk and mingle because they're a gathering point of a party.

Fondues and dips share sociability; they are meant to be shared. Famed American food writer M.F.K. Fisher wrote that "sharing food with another human being is an intimate act that should not be indulged in lightly." And isn't personal connection what these foods are all about?

How This Book Is Organized

The book is divided into five parts:

Part 1, "Fondue Fundamentals," teaches you everything you need to know to master fondues and hot dips. It begins with a chapter detailing how to choose and care for fondue pots and other necessary accessories—or how to recycle some pans you might already own as fondue pots. It also gives you some guidance on how to plan a fondue fiesta along with the table etiquette particular to fondue. The next chapter encompasses selection and handling of frequently used foods and lists creative ideas for foods to dip. It ends with a section on food safety—an important concept regardless of what you're cooking.

Part 2, "Say Cheese!" takes you back to the birth of fondue and then builds on the concept. The first chapter in Part 2 focuses on classic cheese fondue with many variations. You'll find recipes using beer instead of wine and fondues that list many non-Swiss cheeses in the ingredients. Smooth fondues become chunky with vegetables in the next chapter, and Part 2 ends with a chapter of fondue recipes that incorporate various meats and seafood.

Part 3, "Tabletop Cooking," expands the definition of fondues to include a whole new category—ones that are actually cooked at the table in either simmering broth or hot oil. These fondues benefit from being dipped into some delicious sauce after cooking. Recipes for a wide range of easy sauces complete the chapters in Part 3.

Part 4, "Dippity Do!" introduces you to the incredible variety of hot dips that are the mainstay of casual entertaining. Dips are thicker than fondues, which is why you scoop them out with sturdy foods rather than delicately dipping foods into them. I've given all vegetarian recipes in one chapter, and a few are even vegan. Part 4 continues to explore dips with recipes that include meats and seafood.

Part 5, "Decadent Desserts," proves that you're always smart when you leave room for dessert. Check out the chapter devoted to chocolate fondues. This is where dessert fondues all began, and you'll find luscious melted chocolate paired with many flavor accents. Dessert flavors such as caramel and butterscotch and textures such as crunchy nuts are also featured, and Part 5 concludes with fondue recipes featuring a rainbow of colorful and delicious fruits.

At the end you'll find some useful appendixes. A glossary adds to your knowledge of cooking lingo and an appendix of charts helps you convert measurements to the metric system.

Extras

In every chapter you'll find boxes that give you extra information that is either helpful, interesting, or both.

Dip Tips

These boxes are full of cooking tips. Some are specific to the recipes they accompany; others boost your general cooking skills or give you ideas for food presentation.

Fondue Facts

Check out these boxes for amusing tidbits of food history. They're fun to read and share with friends, and they'll make you sound like a real gourmet.

Dip-Tionary

Cooking has a language all its own, and some of the terms and ingredients can be intimidating if you don't know what they mean. Look to these boxes for technique and ingredient definitions.

Fon-Don'ts

It's always a good idea to be alerted to potential problems in advance. Boxes labeled Fon-Don'ts provide just such a warning, either about cooking in general or the recipe in particular.

Acknowledgments

Writing a book is a solitary endeavor, but its publication is always a team effort. My thanks go to …

Michele Wells of Alpha Books and Ed Claflin, my agent, for proposing the project.

Christy Wagner, Megan Douglass, and Emily Garner for their expert and eagle-eyed editing.

My many friends, especially Constance Brown and Kenn Speiser, who were beginning to wonder if fondue forks were going to be permanently set on my dining table.

Tigger-Cat Brown and Patches-Kitten Brown, my furry companions, who kept me company for endless hours at the computer and approved all seafood recipes.

Special Thanks to the Technical Reviewer

The Complete Idiot's Guide to Fondues and Hot Dips was reviewed by an expert who double-checked the accuracy of what you'll learn here, to help us ensure that this book gives you everything you need to know about making fabulous fondues and fun hot dips. Special thanks are extended to Lisa Vislocky.

Trademarks

All terms mentioned in this book that are known to be or are suspected of being trademarks or service marks have been appropriately capitalized. Alpha Books and Penguin Group (USA) Inc. cannot attest to the accuracy of this information. Use of a term in this book should not be regarded as affecting the validity of any trademark or service mark.

Part 1

Fondue Fundamentals

This part could also be called "Everything You Ever Wanted to Know About Fondue but Were Afraid to Ask"—and that begins with picking the pot. It can be a special fondue pot, or it can be that chafing dish you packed away years ago. In addition to the pot, other accessories and some eating etiquette lead to a successful fondue fiesta.

There are two facets to cooking fondue: what's in the pot and what food gets dipped into the pot. In Chapter 2, you learn about both.

Chapter 1

Setting the Scene

In This Chapter

- The history of fondue
- Selecting or improvising a fondue pot
- Serving a fondue dinner

Fondue is perfect for eating with a group of friends and family members. If you're dining alone and want crusty bread and gooey cheese, chances are you'd make a grilled cheese sandwich, not a pot of cheese fondue. Fondues are meant to be shared and slowly savored.

In this chapter, you learn about the history of fondues and also how to improvise a fondue pot with what you have on hand. You'll also read about the proper fondue serving and eating etiquette along with some serving safety information.

The Original Melting Pot

The fondue family tree has its roots deep in the mountains of Switzerland. The word *fondue* comes from the French word *fondre*, which means "to melt." The culinary practice of fondue began in the Canton of Neuchâtel in the early eighteenth century, where both cheese and wine were important agricultural industries.

Traditional Swiss fondue specifies at least two cheeses to add complexity to the taste, and each canton of the country has its own style. In eastern Switzerland, hard cider is used in place of the traditional wine; in Vaud, roasted garlic is added to the fondue rather than merely scenting the pot with a clove before cooking.

A few conflicting theories exist about the history of meat fondue—or more precisely *Fondue Bourguignonne*—but both place the parentage in Burgundy. In one theory, the dish was started in the region's famed vineyards as a way to feed the laborers harvesting grapes; another history pins the invention on a monk.

Lighter and healthier broth fondues are an example of *fusion* cuisine. Although not part of European tradition, these fondues are part of many Asian cultures. In China, an elaborate device called a hot pot is used.

Fondue Facts

While fondue credit is often given to the Swiss, the ancient Greeks might be able to claim the moniker. Homer's *Iliad* (*Song XI*) contains a recipe that's clearly a fondue. The passage discusses a blend of goat cheese with Pramnos wine and flour.

Dip-Tionary

Fusion cooking, blending cooking styles and ingredients from disparate cuisines, became popular in the 1980s. Most common is using Asian ingredients in classic French cooking, but fusion can also be the opposite—adding European seasonings to Asian dishes.

A Panoply of Pots

If you're going to serve fondue on any sort of regular basis, chances are you'll want to invest in a fondue pot. In the 1970s, only two choices were available: ceramic pots for cheese and desserts and metal pots for oil. Today, the choices are basically the same but with a lot more bells and whistles. If you're going to serve both categories of fondue, you should probably have both types of pot. If you're going to buy just one pot, make it a metal one. You can't boil oil in a ceramic pot, but you can serve cheese in a metal pot over a very low flame.

The traditional pot for cheese fondue is called a *caquelon* or *câclon*. These low and wide fondue pots are traditionally made from earthenware, but you can also find them made of glazed ceramic or enameled iron. These pots are heavy to help promote even heat distribution so the cheese doesn't scorch. Some models have an additional heat diffuser—a metal plate with small holes that sits between the fondue pot and the heat source.

A caquelon fondue pot is also perfect for dessert fondues, especially those made with chocolate, which can scorch even more easily than cheese. However, because of the size of the pot, you'd need to make a lot of dessert fondue to fill it with enough liquid to facilitate dipping. The best choices for dessert fondues are the small caquelons specifically for des-

Fondue Facts

Some fondue fanatics believe the only beverage that should be consumed with cheese fondue is a red wine, served at room temperature, and that water should never be consumed lest it make the cheese congeal in the stomach. I've never found this to be true, though.

serts. Dip-size slow cookers work well, too. These hold 2 cups liquid, perfect for dessert for six or cheese for two diners.

Fondue pots intended for oil or broth are always made of metal and are wider at the bottom than at the top, with a taller profile to allow the oil or broth to stay hot.

Relatively new to the market are electric, thermostatically controlled pots. Many of them are a cross between the two traditional shapes; they're deeper than a classic cheese pot but wider than a classic metal pot. My experience with them has been excellent, and there's no pesky fuel to consider (see the next section for more on fuel). I did find that the cord is never long enough to reach even the side of the table let alone a plug, though, so you might want to pick up an extension cord, too, if you purchase one of these pots.

Fueling the Fire

Unless you opt for the electric fondue pot, you'll need some sort of heat source to keep the fondue bubbly. I'm not talking about sticking a votive candle under the pot, either (except maybe if you're heating a chocolate fondue in a thin pot); it won't produce enough heat. You need a fondue burner.

The common fondue burner has three pieces:

- A burner unit to hold the fuel
- A fitted cover with adjustable vents to control the size of the fire
- An extinguisher for when the party's over

The burners vary little, but the fuels vary a lot. Of course there's Sterno, the gel fuel that comes in small tins or bottles. It's fine for cheese, but it's not as good for oil or broth. An alternative to gel fuel is alcohol, which burns hotter than gel but is also messier to use.

The new kid on the fuel-source block is the butane burner. These burners have a sleek design that holds miniature canisters and enable you to set the flame as precisely as you would set the gas burner on your kitchen range.

Fon-Don'ts

Just because you have one type of burner for another utensil and a pot the same shape as a fondue pot, don't try to rig up a stand. Remember that you're literally playing with fire.

The best place to find fuels for fondue burners is a hardware store. These fuels are widely used for other appliances, so they are often in stock. You could also check out the camping department of full-service department stores.

Fondue Pot Considerations

When you're shopping for a fondue pot, keep these points in mind:

- ◆ Unless you're buying an electric pot that works with all kinds of fondue, select the appropriate pot for your fondue.
- ◆ Be sure the pot sits firmly on the stand to minimize the chance of tipping.
- ◆ See if the manufacturer's instructions indicate that the pot can be heated directly on the stove. It's much easier to create the fondue right in the pot and then transport the pot to the stand.
- ◆ Check to be sure the pot is dishwasher-safe if that convenience is important to you. Many ceramic pots are not.
- ◆ If the pot is intended for oil and broth fondues, check to be sure it has a notched metal lip on the edge to keep diners' forks from falling into one another.

New Uses for Old Friends

If you want to try fondue a few times before investing in a dedicated pot, some of the pans you've bought for other purposes might do the trick.

For cheese or dessert fondue, try your slow cooker. It would take forever to melt the cheese in a slow cooker, but once the fondue is created, the slow cooker certainly keeps it hot enough to eat if set on high.

Another alternative is a chafing dish. Perhaps you have one that's brought out for parties and that's small enough for fondue. Chafing dishes use the same fuel sources as fondue pots, and the shape is similar.

If you have a small electric deep fryer you're all set for oil and broth fondues—you have the pot and the heating element all in one.

Gadgets Galore

Every cook has a number of favorite kitchen gadgets, and some are more important than others for making fondues and hot dips. Here are some I use often:

Food processor My food processor has a dedicated spot in the dishwasher because I use it nearly every day. Get one that holds at least 2 quarts, or you'll be wasting time with multiple batches. Although most accessories are superfluous, I use the shredding disc for cheeses and the slicing disc for vegetables as often as the steel blade.

Zester This gizmo, which resembles a vegetable peeler with small holes in the top, makes removing the *zest* from citrus fruits an effortless task.

Instant-read thermometer This does just what it promises, and it's a sure-fire way to ensure that your custard isn't going to curdle. Once inserted into food, an instant-read thermometer produces an accurate reading in about 5 seconds.

Deep-fry thermometer If you're making an oil fondue, it's really important to know the temperature of the oil before removing it from the stove, and this thermometer does double-duty because it also takes the temperature of sugar syrup when you're making caramel or other desserts.

Flat-bottom whisk This utensil makes cooking flour for a *roux* a dream job. It has an angled handle and covers the entire surface of the saucepan. Rounded balloon whisks are great for whisking, but a flat-bottom whisk is what you want for sauces.

Balloon whisks Sturdy whisks to add cheese to liquid and keep the liquid moving are the secret to smooth fondue. While some people say the cheese should be added with a wooden spoon, I've never found them as effective.

Box grater For small amounts of cheese, or if your food processor in the dishwasher, a sturdy box grater can come in handy. Depending on the cheese, you can use either the large holes or the slicing side.

Dip-Tionary

Zest is the outermost layer of the skin of citrus fruits, where all the aromatic oils are located. It's important to remove only the colored portion, as the white pith beneath it is very bitter. **Roux** (pronounced as in *kangaroo*) is the French term for the mixture of fat and flour that's cooked before being used as thickener for a sauce. The purpose of cooking the roux is so the flour will not give the resulting sauce a "floury" taste.

Serving Strategy

Fondues are easy to make, yes, but you must keep a few other considerations in mind before you invite friends for a fondue fête.

Consider first your table shape and size. A long rectangular dining table isn't as conducive to dipping as a round table, but if that's what's in your dining room, there are ways around it, such as using two pots—one at either end—rather than one in the middle. The other idea is to buy a round fiberboard flip-top that transforms an inexpensive card table into a round table for six.

Fon-Don'ts

Fondue is not a neat meal, so don't use Grandma's best linens on the table.

Fondue Facts

In Switzerland, serving fondue has its own set of customs. If a man drops his bread cube into the pot, he is supposed to buy the next pot or a round of drinks, assuming the diners are at a restaurant. If a woman loses the bread, she has her choice of which man she'd like to kiss.

Next, do you have enough room on your table for all the accouterments that are part and parcel of fondue? Is there room for a basket of bread? If you're serving an oil or broth fondue, do you have enough small bowls for sauces and platters for the food prior to cooking?

If not, the best thing to do is to create individual dishes for each diner in the kitchen and serve them as you would any plated entrée. If you're serving sauces, you can then pass large bowls around the table and diners can ladle them onto their plates.

The Pot's Pals

You have the fondue and dipping foods, you've considered the size and shape of your table and arranged accordingly. You're ready to dig in, right? Not so fast. What are your diners going to hold the dipping food with? Their fingers? In the hot sauce or oil? Nope. You need long-handled forks, or something similar, for this. But fondue pot manufacturers help you out with this: most pots come with a set of six forks (that's why the recipes in this book are written for that number).

Fon-Don'ts

Bamboo skewers can be used for cheese and dessert fondues, but never serve bamboo skewers with oil or broth fondues. They are not sturdy enough to withstand the heat.

Fondue forks are longer than table forks, and they have two sharp prongs for spearing food. They're almost always metal, and if you're serving oil or broth fondue, they should have heatproof handles such as wood or plastic.

Another good accessory to have, especially if you're serving an oil or broth fondue, is a Lazy Susan. Be sure to warn your guests about spinning it too rapidly when sharing the sauce bowls. You don't want that hot oil or cheese splattering all over your diners!

Pleasing Miss Manners

Many people think of eating fondue as exposure to a Petri dish of germs, and that shouldn't be a worry. Communal eating is as sanitary as any other type of dining style if certain safety practices are followed.

Most fondue forks come with colored buttons at the end so people can identify their own fork. But be sure to tell your diners that the fondue fork itself should never transport food from the pot to their mouths. The colored ends indicate which fork they should monitor and retrieve from the pot to bring the cooked food to their plate—not their mouth. To help your friends and family master fondue etiquette, set each table setting with traditional cutlery—knife, fork, and teaspoon—in addition to the fondue fork. It might help to remind everyone that the purpose of the fondue fork is for transportation only and to use the other utensils for consuming the cooked food.

Fondue Facts

We might think of the French as the ultimate gastronomes, but it was an Italian who introduced table cutlery to France. Marie de'Medici brought it with her as part of her trousseau when she married King Henry II in the fifteenth century.

But what about "double dipping," you ask? The best solution to this sticky problem is to cut food into small enough cubes that they are truly one bite.

While double-dipping is a no-no, a discrete twirl or tap before moving morsels from the fondue pot to the plate is not only proper but also advantageous. If you're eating a cheese or dessert fondue, this twirl allows excess fondue to fall back into the pot rather than on to the table. If you're eating an oil or broth fondue, this move allows the food to cool slightly as well.

Safe Serving

When you have a live flame on your table, there's always a certain risk involved. Here are some tips on fondue safety:

Place the pot on a baking stone, heavy trivet, or ceramic platter. Never put a fondue pot directly on a wooden table.

Always use the type of fuel specified by the manufacturer. Gel burners are similar in appearance to alcohol burners, but the internal structure is different and using the wrong fuel can cause a fire.

Light the burner with a long match, not a lighter to keep the flame far from your fingers.

Never refill the burner while it's lit. Most burners last more than 1 hour per filling, so if you think the party will last longer than that, purchase an additional burner.

Keep the burner cover handy at all times should you need to smother the flame. It's also a good idea to keep a fire extinguisher at a close distance.

Be sure any lit candles are tall enough so diners won't encounter them when reaching in and out of the fondue pot.

Fondue Facts

Hard-core fondue eaters indulge in what's called the *coup de milieu,* dipping bread cubes into a glass of kirsch before dipping them into the cheese. This supposedly aids in digestion.

The Least You Need to Know

◆ Cheese fondue originated in Switzerland in the eighteenth century. Meat fondue started in the Burgundy region of France during the Middle Ages.

◆ Traditional fondue pots come in two different shapes. One is intended for cheese and dessert fondue, and the other is for oil and broth dishes.

◆ Appliances such as slow cookers and chafing dishes can do double-duty as fondue pots.

◆ Guests should be informed that it's not good manners to put their fondue fork in their mouths and then back into the fondue pot.

2

Prepping the Parts

In This Chapter

- ◆ A guide to cheese
- ◆ Ingredients to keep on hand
- ◆ Foods to dip
- ◆ Tips on keeping food safe

Cooking requires both hardware and software. The hardware is the fondue pot and other accessories I covered in Chapter 1. The software is food, and that's what this chapter is all about. Here you'll learn about cheeses, how to select them, and how to handle them for fondues and hot dips.

But there's more in the supermarket than a cheese counter, so we won't stop there. This chapter also contains shopping lists of ingredients commonly used in fondue recipes. If you stock these foods in your pantry, you can often whip up quick fondues when guests pop by unexpectedly.

Cheese 101

There are literally hundreds of cheeses produced around the world. The critical factors in determining a cheese's distinctive characteristics are…

- ◆ The kind of milk used. It's not only cows that produce cheese-making milk; sheep's milk and goat's milk are also used for countless cheeses. In addition to the type of cheese the fat content of the cheese is also important.
- ◆ The coagulation methods, cutting, cooking, forming the curd, the type of culture, salting, and the ripening method.

Creation of Curd

Most cheeses are the products of coagulated milk. This process produces curds, which are then drained from the liquid containing another milk protein, whey.

During cheese making, *lactobacillus* cultures, i.e., bacteria, convert lactose into lactic acid. This coagulates the milk's protein into curds. Salt is added to all cheeses other than fresh cheese.

Whys of Whey

Curds may be eaten immediately as fresh, nonripened cheese. For ripened or aged cheese, the curd is further treated by selected bacteria, mold, yeast, or a combination of ripening agents and then aged under carefully controlled conditions

Some cheeses are hung to remove excess moisture (ricotta), while many others are pressed. Whole milk, low-fat milk, skim milk, or any combination may be used to make cheese. But fondues are best with the minimum fat content being that of whole milk and the higher the fat content the better.

Substitution Solutions

Regardless of the type of cheese you're melting, the quality is all important to the success of a fondue or hot dip. At times, the cheese specified in a recipe may not be available in your market. But that's no reason to deny yourself if you fancy a fondue. Cheeses fall into basic categories that can be substituted successfully for one another. These categories are defined by primarily the texture of the cheese.

Hard cheeses are cooked, pressed, and aged for long periods (usually at least 2 years) until they're hard and dry. These cheeses are generally used for grating. Among the more well-known of this genre are Parmesan and pecorino, and both are universally available.

Semihard cheeses are firm but not usually crumbly. They have been cooked and pressed but not aged as long as those in the hard cheese category. The bulk of cheeses used for fondue are in this category, including Gruyère, Emmenthal, Jarlsberg, cheddar, Edam, and American Swiss cheese.

Semisoft cheeses are pressed but can be either cooked or uncooked. Their texture is sliceable but soft. This is the group where you'll find Gouda, Monterey Jack, Asiago, Bel Paese, fontina, Havarti, and Muenster.

Soft-ripened cheeses are neither cooked nor pressed. Instead, they're dipped or sprayed with a bacteria that ripens them from the outside in. In this category you'll find Brie, Camembert, Brillat-Savarin, Explorateur, Vacherin, and St. André.

Fondue Facts

While most cheeses are named for the place they're made, Brillat-Savarin immortalized famed French food writer Anthelme Brillat-Savarin (1755–1826). His noted work, *The Physiology of Taste*, contains such great lines as "tell me what you eat, and I will tell you what you are," and "the discovery of a new dish does more for human happiness than the discovery of a new star."

Blue-veined cheeses are lumped together regardless of texture because their flavors are similar. These cheeses are inoculated or sprayed with spores of the molds *Penicillium roqueforti* or *Penicillium glaucum*. Some of these cheeses are punctured with holes to ensure that the mold will penetrate during the aging period. The result of these painstaking efforts are cheeses with veins or pockets of flavorful blue or green mold, such as Italian Gorgonzola, English Stilton, French Roquefort, blue de Bresse, and American Maytag blue.

Pasta filata, which means "spun paste," is another special-processed cheese from Italy. These cheeses are made using a special technique whereby the curd is given a hot whey bath, kneaded, and stretched to the desired pliable consistency. Mozzarella, provolone, and caciocavallo are in this group.

Grating to Greatness

Although some cheeses can be sliced into thin slices or shredded to make a fondue or hot dip, unless otherwise noted, grating is the most efficient way to prepare cheese for melting.

The easiest way to grate is to use a food processor fitted with a steel blade. Cut the cheese into 1-inch cubes if it's semisoft like Emmenthal and $\frac{1}{2}$-inch cubes if it's hard like Parmesan. Turn on the processor and drop the cubes through the feed tube slowly. Never let the work bowl become more than $\frac{1}{3}$ full, and stop the machine if the cheese is beginning to form a ball rather than remain as separate particles.

It requires more elbow grease, but the large holes on a box grater are the tried-and-true way of grating cheese. If you spray the front and back with a nonflavored vegetable oil spray, the cheese won't stick and will be easier to grate.

Fon-Don'ts

Never, ever used pregrated cheeses for a fondue or hot dip. The flavor of cheese begins to dissipate within moments of grating it, and the basic quality of pre-grated cheeses isn't high in the first place.

Cheese is easier to grate if it's chilled. This is even true for hard cheeses like Parmesan, and it's especially true for cheeses like mozzarella. One exception is the soft-ripened cheeses like Brie. Those should be softened to facilitate removing the rind.

Dippers That Dazzle

So far our exploration of food has focused on what goes into the pot, but now it's time to showcase dippers for both fondues and hot dips. I give suggestions with each recipe, but some general pointers when choosing foods will enhance your total eating experience.

In general, foods to dip should not compete in flavor with what's in the pot; the two should work in tandem to present a delicious eating experience that makes the whole more than the sum of its parts.

Fondue Facts

Dips were known by other names around the world for centuries, but their popularity in this country only came in the twentieth century. According to accounts, Mrs. Woodrow Wilson served a sort of clam dip at the White House, and it was the legendary James Beard whose book *Hors d'Oeuvres and Canapés* appeared in 1940 and cemented the genre.

Fondues and hot dips have different requirements for foods to dip. For fondues, dippers should be supple enough to stay on the fork without breaking apart but sturdy enough that they don't fall into the fondue pot. Supersturdy is the key for hot dip dippers. That's why you don't see potato chips listed—they break apart too easily when they hit a hot temperature. Save potato and other vegetable chips for cold dips or snacking.

Choice Carbs

The traditional dipper for cheese fondue is a cube of bread, and some sort of crusty bread should be served with any cheese fondue. But you don't have to limit yourself to a French baguette or its Italian equivalent. Whole-grain breads, pumpernickel, focaccia, and rye bread are all great. Take your cue from the flavors in the fondue.

Other types of carbohydrates can be served alongside the bread basket, too. Small cooked pastas such as tortellini are dynamite for dipping, as are slices of potato. If you'd like it with a cheese sauce, then it works to dip in a cheese fondue.

Versatile Veggies

Some vegetables are fine raw for dipping, such as carrots, celery, cucumber spears, and slices of fresh fennel. But other vegetables have both a more pleasing color and texture if they're cooked briefly in boiling water and then drained. The process is called *blanching*, and it's easy to do.

Fondue Facts

The English word **blanch** comes from the French word *blancher,* which means "to whiten." The term is now used for any short preliminary cooking (usually of fruits and vegetables). Peaches and tomatoes are blanched to ease peeling.

Dip Tips

If you have a manual ice-cream machine with a freezable insert, use it for chilling vegetables without additional ice. Once the basket is frozen, you can add tap water. It will last for many rounds of blanched vegetables.

The time-honored way to blanch is to bring a large pot of salted water to a boil (you want the water to come back to a boil as quickly as possible after you add the veggies). Add the vegetables, and let them boil for no more than 2 minutes, depending on size and texture. Sturdy broccoli or cauliflower florets should go for the whole 2 minutes; delicate snow peas should boil for 30 seconds. Then drain them in a colander.

If you have a number of vegetables to blanch, you can cook them sequentially, beginning with the one with the lightest flavor because some flavor does enter the water. Scoop out the vegetables using a slotted spoon or wire mesh skimmer and then add the next batch.

The other way to blanch is in the microwave. Place the vegetables in a shallow microwave-safe dish, add $\frac{1}{4}$ cup water, and cover the dish completely with plastic wrap. Microwave on high for 30 seconds to 2 minutes, depending on the quantity and sturdiness of the vegetable.

After cooking, for both methods, plunge the vegetables into ice water to stop the cooking action and set the color. You can use the same batch of water; just keep adding ice. Then pat the vegetables dry with paper towels and store them refrigerated in plastic bags for up to a day.

Safety First!

The first and most important requirement for good cooking is knowing the basic rules of food safety. This begins during the trip to the supermarket and ends after leftovers are refrigerated or frozen at the end of a meal. Fondues and hot dips might be casual food, but it's still food, and *casual* doesn't mean *careless*.

Safe Shopping

The layout of most supermarkets funnels you into the produce section first, but that's not the best place to start. Begin your shopping with the shelf-stable items from the center, then go to produce, and end with the other refrigerated and frozen sections.

Never buy meat or poultry in a package that's torn and leaking. And it's a good idea to place all meats and poultry in the disposable plastic bags available in the produce department and, increasingly, in the meat department as well.

Check the "sell-by" and "use-by" dates, and never purchase food that exceeds them. For the trip home, it's a good idea to carry an insulated cooler in the back of your car if it's hot outside or if the perishable items will be out of refrigeration for more than 1 hour. In hot weather, many seafood departments will provide some crushed ice in a separate bag for the fish.

Dip Tips_____

If you have any questions about food safety, the U.S. Department of Agriculture (USDA) is the place to turn for information, especially the Food Safety Inspection Service. Check out the USDA's website, www.fsis.usda.gov, for a wealth of information in a very user-friendly format.

Banishing Bacteria

Fruits and vegetables can contain some bacteria, but it's far more likely that the culprits will grow on meat, poultry, and seafood. Store these foods on the bottom shelves of your refrigerator so their juices cannot accidentally drip on other foods. And keep these foods refrigerated until just before they're either cooked or brought to the table. It's fine to do an artful arrangement of raw meats in advance for an oil or broth fondue, but keep that platter separate from the one holding vegetables, and keep it refrigerated.

Avoiding Cross-Contamination

Cleanliness is not only next to godliness, it's also the key to food safety. Wash your hands often while you're cooking, especially after touching raw food. And never touch raw food and then cooked food without washing your hands in between.

> **Dip Tips**
>
> A good way to prevent food-borne illness is by selecting the right cutting board. Wooden boards might be attractive, but you can never get them as clean as plastic boards that can be run through the dishwasher. Even with plastic boards, it's best to use one for only cooked food and foods such as vegetables that are not prone to contain bacteria, and another one devoted to raw meats, poultry, and fish.

The "cooked food and raw food shall never meet" precept extends beyond the cook's hands. Clean cutting boards, knives, and kitchen counters often. Or if you have the space, section off your countertops for raw foods and cooked foods, as many restaurant kitchens do. Don't place cooked foods or raw foods that will remain uncooked (such as salad) on cutting boards that have been used to cut raw meat, poultry, or fish. Bacteria from raw animal proteins can contaminate the other foods.

The Least You Need to Know

- Cheese can be made from the milk of cows, sheep, and goats.
- Keep dried herbs and spices in cool, dark places to preserve their color and flavor.
- Vegetables such as broccoli, cauliflower, and snow peas have better color and texture if they're blanched in boiling water.
- To ensure food safety, cooked food should never come into contact with raw food, including on hands and on cutting boards or platters.

Part 2

Say Cheese!

Gooey, rich, bubbling cheese fondue is how the fondue family was born centuries ago in Switzerland.

The recipes in Part 2 all contain melted cheese. But that's where the similarity ends. The purely classic mixtures are detailed in Chapter 3, along with a chart for cheese substitutions.

But there's a whole world of cheese fondues beyond the basics, and that's what you also find in this part. The recipes in Chapter 4 include a cornucopia of vegetables with cheese, and in Chapter 5, other protein sources—from meats to seafoods—become the supporting players.

Classic Combinations

In This Chapter

- ◆ Classic Swiss fondue and its first cousins
- ◆ Fondues made with wines and beers
- ◆ Smooth cheese fondues flavored with herbs and spices

What comes to mind when you say "fondue" to most people is a bubbly caldron of hot cheese into which food—typically cubes of bread—are dipped. You'll find this classic Swiss fondue among the recipes in this chapter, but there's a lot more.

These recipes are united by the fact that they're smooth rather than chunky, and they specify that the cheese is melted in some sort of alcoholic beverage. But that's where the similarities end. In these pages you'll find fondues made with cheeses from a United Nations of countries and blended with beverages from light wines to heady liqueurs.

Liquid Assets

All cheese fondue is somehow related to original Swiss fondue, which uses a light Swiss white wine as the base into which the cheese is melted. But today you have many options for making these dishes.

The main reason for incorporating alcohols into dishes is for flavoring; however, alcohols were originally added to fondues to lower the melting point of cheese, thereby preventing curdling. Contrary to popular belief, although much of the alcohol mixed into any dish dissipates with enough heat exposure, some almost always remains. Always be sure to inform your guests if you've used alcohol in a dish to avoid any allergic reactions or adverse health consequences.

If you don't drink alcohol at all, you could use a nonalcoholic wine or beer instead of the "leaded" variety. You can find these in the supermarket, usually with drink mixers.

Methodical Melting

Cheese fondue is fast food, especially if you've grated the cheese earlier in the day. If you want to jump-start the process that's fine, but keep the grated cheese refrigerated and tightly covered. Cheese has a tendency to dry out quickly and lose its aroma and flavor. Keeping cheese refrigerated after grating also ensures it will stay as separate particles and not form a lump. This is important for the quality of the fondue.

Fondue Facts

Author Clifton Fadiman said it best when he described cheese as "milk's leap toward immortality."

The recipes in this chapter all call for cornstarch as a thickening agent, but that's more for insurance than necessity. A properly made cheese fondue basically holds itself together. That's why it's important to add only a small amount of cheese at a time and stir it in a figure-eight pattern. If you stir it in a circle, the cheese has a tendency to form a ball in the center rather than disperse evenly into the liquid base.

Successful Serving

Cheese scorches easily, which is why ceramic fondue pots are the preferred choice for serving cheese-based fondues. The thickness of the ceramic prevents the heat source underneath from forming a "hot spot" in the center that will burn the cheese directly above it.

If you're using a ceramic fondue pot, give it some help keeping the fondue hot by heating it in a 375°F oven for 30 minutes before adding the liquid fondue. With this heating head start, all you need to keep it hot while your diners dip and nibble away is a small candle.

If your fondue should cool off to the point that it's too thick to twirl the food, don't despair. Just scrape the fondue back into the saucepan you cooked it in, and reheat it until it bubbles again!

Classic Cheese Fondue

| Serves: **6** | Prep time: **15 minutes** | Cook time: **10 minutes** |

1 garlic clove, peeled and halved crosswise

1 ½ cups dry white wine

½ lb. (2 cups) Emmenthal cheese, coarsely grated

½ lb. (2 cups) Gruyère cheese, coarsely grated

2 TB. *kirsch*

1 TB. cornstarch

1. Rub the inside of a heavy 2-quart saucepan with the cut sides of garlic. Discard garlic. Add wine to the pot, and bring to a simmer over medium heat.

2. Add Emmenthal and Gruyère cheeses to wine by ½ cup measures, stirring constantly with a whisk in a figure-eight pattern. Add additional cheese only after the previous addition is melted.

Dip-Tionary

Kirsch, also labeled *kirschwasser,* is a clear, tart cherry brandy distilled from cherry juice and cherry pits. In addition to the characteristic flavor in cheese fondue, kirsch is what's used to flame cherries jubilee.

3. Combine kirsch and cornstarch in a small bowl, and stir to dissolve cornstarch. Add to fondue, and bring to a simmer, stirring constantly. Cook over low heat for 1 to 2 minutes or until fondue has thickened.

4. Transfer fondue to a fondue pot or other pot with a heat source, and serve with crusty French or Italian bread cubes, steamed broccoli or cauliflower florets, halved or quartered, steamed or oven-roasted new potatoes, cooked tortellini or ravioli, or bite-size pieces of cooked chicken or baked ham.

Three-Cheese Champagne Fondue

| Serves: **6** | Prep time: **15 minutes** | Cook time: **10 minutes** |

1 garlic clove, peeled and halved crosswise

1¼ cups dry (brut) champagne

1 TB. freshly squeezed lemon juice

Pinch ground nutmeg

½ lb. (2 cups) Gruyère cheese, coarsely grated

⅓ lb. (1½ cups) Emmenthal cheese, coarsely grated

⅓ lb. (1½ cups) Brie cheese, rind scraped away and finely diced

2 TB. brandy or Cognac

1 TB. cornstarch

1. Rub the inside of a heavy 2-quart saucepan with the cut sides of garlic. Discard garlic. Add champagne, lemon juice, and nutmeg to the pot, and bring to a simmer over medium heat.

2. Add Gruyère, Emmenthal, and Brie cheeses to champagne by ½ cup measures, stirring constantly with a whisk in a figure-eight pattern. Add additional cheese only after the previous addition is melted.

Dip Tips

Lemon juice is added to many fondue recipes because the acid content enhances the cheese's ability to melt evenly. Some cheeses, such as Brie, always need lemon juice to melt smoothly.

3. Combine brandy and cornstarch in a small bowl, and stir to dissolve cornstarch. Add to fondue, and bring to a simmer, stirring constantly. Cook over low heat for 1 to 2 minutes or until fondue has thickened.

4. Transfer fondue to a fondue pot or other pot with a heat source, and serve with crusty French or Italian bread cubes, steamed broccoli or cauliflower florets, halved or quartered, steamed or oven-roasted new potatoes, cooked tortellini or ravioli, or bite-size pieces of cooked chicken or baked ham.

Italian Cheese Fondue

Serves: **6**	*Prep time:* **15 minutes**	*Cook time:* **10 minutes**

1 garlic clove, peeled and halved

1½ cups dry Italian white wine, such as Pinot Grigio

¾ lb. (3 cups) Gorgonzola cheese, coarsely grated

½ lb. (2 cups) whole milk mozzarella cheese, coarsely grated

1 TB. *grappa* or other Italian brandy

1 TB. cornstarch

1. Rub the inside of a heavy 2-quart saucepan with the cut sides of garlic. Discard garlic. Add wine to the pot, and bring to a simmer over medium heat.

2. Add Gorgonzola and mozzarella cheeses to wine by ½ cup measures, constantly with a whisk in a figure-eight pattern. Add additional cheese only after the previous addition is melted.

3. Combine grappa and cornstarch in a small bowl, and stir to dissolve cornstarch. Add to fondue, and bring to a simmer, stirring constantly. Cook over low heat for 1 to 2 minutes or until fondue has thickened.

4. Transfer fondue to a fondue pot or other pot with a heat source, and serve with crusty French or Italian bread cubes, flour or corn tortilla squares, steamed broccoli or cauliflower florets, halved or quartered, steamed or oven-roasted new potatoes, cooked tortellini or ravioli, or bite-size pieces of cooked chicken or roast pork.

Dip-Tionary

Grappa is a clear Italian liqueur distilled from the grape skins and seeds left in the wine press after the juice is released. It's high in alcohol, and there's a lot of stylistic variation depending on the species of grape.

English Cheddar and Beer Fondue (Welsh Rarebit)

Serves: **6**	*Prep time:* **15 minutes**	*Cook time:* **10 minutes**

1 (12-oz.) can lager beer

1 TB. prepared mustard, preferably English

2 tsp. paprika

½ tsp. cayenne

1 lb. (4 cups) sharp cheddar cheese, coarsely grated

1 TB. cold water

1 TB. cornstarch

Salt and freshly ground black pepper to taste

1. Combine beer, mustard, paprika, and cayenne in a heavy 2-quart saucepan, and stir well. Bring to a simmer over medium heat.

2. Add cheddar cheese to beer by ½ cup measures, stirring constantly with a whisk in a figure-eight pattern. Add additional cheese only after the previous addition is melted.

3. Combine water and cornstarch in a small bowl, and stir to dissolve cornstarch. Add to fondue, and bring to a simmer, stirring constantly. Cook over low heat for 1 to 2 minutes or until fondue has thickened. Season to taste with salt and pepper.

4. Transfer fondue to a fondue pot or other pot with a heat source, and serve with crusty bread cubes, steamed broccoli or cauliflower florets, cherry tomatoes, halved or quartered, steamed or oven-roasted new potatoes, or bite-size pieces of cooked bacon or roast turkey.

Fondue Facts

Welsh Rarebit, sometimes called Welsh Rabbit, is a classic dish served in English pubs for high tea. It consists of cheddar cheese, beer, and seasonings over toast. Unlike afternoon tea, which was for the gentry, high tea was the supper of the working class because their main meal of the day was at noon-time.

Smoked Cheddar and Applejack Fondue

| Serves: **6** | Prep time: **15 minutes** | Cook time: **10 minutes** |

$1\frac{1}{2}$ cups hard apple cider or $1\frac{1}{4}$ cups apple cider and $\frac{1}{4}$ cup apple-jack brandy
1 TB. freshly squeezed lemon juice

$\frac{1}{4}$ tsp. ground cinnamon
$1\frac{1}{4}$ lb. (5 cups) smoked cheddar cheese, coarsely grated
3 TB. applejack brandy
1 TB. cornstarch

1. Combine hard cider, lemon juice, and cinnamon in a heavy 2-quart saucepan, and stir well. Bring to a simmer over medium heat.

2. Add cheddar cheese to cider by $\frac{1}{2}$ cup measures, stirring constantly with a whisk in a figure-eight pattern. Add additional cheese only after the previous addition is melted.

3. Combine applejack brandy and cornstarch in a small bowl, and stir to dissolve cornstarch. Add to fondue, and bring to a simmer, stirring constantly. Cook over low heat for 1 to 2 minutes or until fondue has thickened.

4. Transfer fondue to a fondue pot or other pot with a heat source, and serve with crusty bread cubes, fresh apple or pear slices, halved or quartered, steamed or oven-roasted new potatoes, or bite-size pieces of cooked chicken or baked ham.

Fon-Don'ts

You can cut up the apples up to a few hours in advance, but toss them with lemon juice to prevent them from discoloring to an unappealing brown.

Dutch Gouda Fondue (*Kaaspott*)

| Serves: **6** | Prep time: **15 minutes** | Cook time: **10 minutes** |

1 garlic clove, peeled and halved crosswise

1 ½ cups dry white wine

2 tsp. freshly squeezed lemon juice

Pinch ground nutmeg

1 lb. (4 cups) aged Gouda cheese, rind scraped off and coarsely grated

½ lb. (2 cups) young Gouda cheese, rind scraped off and coarsely grated

2 TB. gin

1 TB. cornstarch

Freshly ground black pepper to taste

1. Rub the inside of a heavy 2-quart saucepan with the cut sides of garlic. Discard garlic. Add wine, lemon juice, and nutmeg to the pot, and bring to a simmer over medium heat.

2. Add aged Gouda and young Gouda cheeses to wine by ½ cup measures, stirring constantly with a whisk in a figure-eight pattern. Add additional cheese only after the previous addition is melted.

3. Combine gin and cornstarch in a small bowl, and stir to dissolve cornstarch. Add to fondue, and bring to a simmer, stirring constantly. Cook over low heat for 1 to 2 minutes or until fondue has thickened. Season to taste with pepper.

Dip-Tionary

Pinch is a term used for the amount of a dry ingredient that can be held between the tips of the thumb and forefinger of one hand. The smallest standard measuring spoon is ¼ teaspoon; a pinch is far less.

4. Transfer fondue to a fondue pot or other pot with a heat source, and serve with crusty pumpernickel or rye bread cubes, steamed broccoli or cauliflower florets, halved or quartered, steamed, or oven-roasted new potatoes, cooked tortellini or ravioli, or bite-size pieces of cooked chicken or baked ham.

Jalapeño Jack and Corona Fondue

| Serves: **6** | Prep time: **15 minutes** | Cook time: **10 minutes** |

1 garlic clove, peeled and halved crosswise

1 (12-oz.) bottle Corona or other beer

¼ to ½ tsp. cayenne

1 lb. (4 cups) *Jalapeño Monterey Jack* cheese, coarsely grated

3 TB. tequila

1 TB. cornstarch

1. Rub the inside of a heavy 2-quart saucepan with the cut sides of garlic. Discard garlic. Add beer and cayenne to the pot, and bring to a simmer over medium heat.

2. Add jalapeño Monterey Jack cheese to beer by ½ cup measures, stirring constantly with a whisk in a figure-eight pattern. Add additional cheese only after the previous addition is melted.

3. Combine tequila and cornstarch in a small bowl, and stir to dissolve cornstarch. Add to fondue, and bring to a simmer, stirring constantly. Cook over low heat for 1 to 2 minutes or until fondue has thickened.

4. Transfer fondue to a fondue pot or other pot with a heat source, and serve with crusty French or Italian bread cubes, flour or corn tortilla squares, steamed broccoli or cauliflower florets, halved or quartered, steamed or oven-roasted new potatoes, cooked tortellini or ravioli, or bite-size pieces of cooked chicken or roast pork.

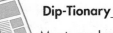 **Dip-Tionary**_____

Monterey Jack cheese was named for its birthplace in Monterey, California. The cheese is similar to a mild Mexican cheese, which is why it's used so often in Mexican recipes. It's buttery in color, semi-soft in texture, and neutral in flavor. It's often found with jalapeño peppers already included, at which time it's called Jalapeño Monterey Jack or just jalapeño Jack.

Curried Cheese Fondue

| Serves: **6** | Prep time: **15 minutes** | Cook time: **10 minutes** |

1 garlic clove, peeled and halved

1½ cups hard apple cider or 1¼ cups apple cider and ¼ cup apple-jack brandy

1 tsp. curry powder

½ lb. (2 cups) Gruyère cheese, coarsely grated

½ lb. (2 cups) smoked Gouda cheese, rind scraped off and coarsely grated

1 TB. *applejack brandy*

1 TB. cornstarch

1. Rub the inside of a heavy 2-quart saucepan with the cut sides of garlic. Discard garlic. Add hard cider and curry powder, and stir well. Bring to a simmer over medium heat.

2. Add Gruyère and smoked Gouda cheeses to cider by ½ cup measures, stirring constantly with a whisk in a figure-eight pattern. Add additional cheese only after the previous addition is melted.

3. Combine applejack brandy and cornstarch in a small bowl, and stir to dissolve cornstarch. Add to fondue, and bring to a simmer, stirring constantly. Cook over low heat for 1 to 2 minutes or until fondue has thickened.

Dip-Tionary

Applejack brandy is distilled from apple cider, and the most famous one in the world is Calvados from the Normandy section of France. In the United States, applejack must be aged for at least 2 years.

4. Transfer fondue to a fondue pot or other pot with a heat source, and serve with crusty French or Italian bread cubes, squares of Indian naan bread, steamed broccoli or cauliflower florets, halved or quartered, steamed or oven-roasted new potatoes, cooked tortellini or ravioli, or bite-size pieces of cooked chicken or roast pork.

Sweet Brie Fondue

| Serves: **6** | Prep time: **15 minutes** | Cook time: **10 minutes** |

1 lb. (4 cups) Brie cheese, softened

1 (3-oz.) pkg. cream cheese, softened

1½ cups Sauternes or other sweet dessert wine

¼ cup firmly packed dark brown sugar

¼ tsp. ground cinnamon

1 TB. triple sec

1 TB. freshly squeezed lemon juice

1 TB. cornstarch

1. Scrape top rind off Brie, and scoop out interior cheese using a spoon. Discard bottom and side rinds. Break cream cheese into 1 tablespoon portions. Place wine, brown sugar, and cinnamon in a heavy 2-quart saucepan, and stir well. Bring to a simmer over medium heat.

2. Add Brie to wine by ½ cup measures, stirring constantly with a whisk in a figure-eight pattern. Add additional cheese only after the previous addition is melted. After Brie has been added, stir in cream cheese by tablespoon measures.

3. Combine triple sec, lemon juice, and cornstarch in a small bowl, and stir to dissolve cornstarch. Add to fondue, and bring to a simmer, stirring constantly. Cook over low heat for 1 to 2 minutes or until fondue has thickened.

4. Transfer fondue to a fondue pot or other pot with a heat source, and serve with crusty French or Italian bread cubes, halved or quartered, steamed or oven-roasted new potatoes, hulled strawberries (halved if large), banana chunks, clementine segments, apple slices, dried apricots, crystallized ginger, or bite-size pieces of cooked chicken or roast pork.

Variation: Camembert or Explorateur cheese can be used instead of Brie.

Fon-Don'ts

Scraping the rind off of soft cheeses like Brie or Camembert might seem like a waste of cheese and an unnecessary step, but it's really important for flavor as well as appearance. The rind lends a harsh note to the fondue.

4

Garden Patch Fondues

In This Chapter

- ◆ Classic fondues with vegetable additions
- ◆ Fondues made with milk and juices
- ◆ Italian fonduta thickened with egg yolks

In cooking, like in music, you have to learn the classics before you start to improvise. The recipes in Chapter 3 covered the basics, so in this chapter and in Chapter 5, I give you recipes for cheese fondue with flavorful additions.

All the recipes in this chapter are vegetarian and contain a cornucopia of ingredients from the garden. In addition to using traditional wine and slightly less-traditional beer as a base, some of these fondues also use milk and vegetable juices.

At the end of this chapter, I give you a trio of recipes called *fondutas* rather than *fondues*. These are Italian in origin and have a silky texture.

Chopping Like a Champ

The fondues in this chapter all have a more complex flavor than a basic fondue because of the addition of ingredients other than cheese. It's important to keep these additions finely chopped so when you dip, you get a full sampling of all the ingredients.

If you have a food processor, use it for chopping, fitted with the steel blade. But don't turn it on and walk away. You want food to be finely chopped but not puréed. Use a quick on-and-off pulsing action, and scrape down the sides of the bowl often as you process.

Fun with Fonduta

Fondutas are silky cheese concoctions differentiated from fondues because they're thickened with egg yolks. This is the same method used to make myriad dishes in both Italian and French cuisine, from pastry creams to hollandaise sauce. The whole idea is that the cheese is melted into the milk and then the egg yolks are added.

You might think it's an unnecessary step to add some of the hot milk to the egg yolks when you're going to add the yolks right into the hot milk. But it's really important to follow that step in the recipe procedure. It's called "tempering" the egg yolks, and it will keep you from getting scrambled eggs rather than a smooth custard.

Cheddar, Roasted Garlic, and Sun-Dried Tomato Fondue

| Serves: **6** | Prep time: **1 hr. 15 min.** | Cook time: **1 hour** |

1 head fresh garlic	1 cup dry white wine
1 TB. olive oil	1 lb. (4 cups) sharp cheddar
2 TB. unsalted butter	cheese, coarsely grated
2 fresh tomatoes, cored, seeded, and finely chopped	1 TB. cold water
	1 TB. cornstarch
¼ cup sun-dried tomatoes packed in oil, drained and finely chopped	Salt and freshly ground black pepper to taste

1. Preheat the oven to 375°F. Cut the top ½ inch off the head of garlic, and rub the cut surface with olive oil. Place garlic on aluminum foil, and wrap the foil around the sides of head, leaving top exposed. Bake garlic for 40 to 50 minutes, or until cloves are soft when the tip of a paring knife is inserted. When garlic is cool enough to handle, break head into cloves. Squeeze cloves to remove pulp, and discard peel. Mash garlic in a small bowl, and set aside. (You can do this up to 2 days in advance and refrigerate it, tightly covered with plastic wrap.)

2. Melt butter in a heavy 2-quart saucepan over medium heat. Add tomatoes and cook, stirring occasionally, for 3 minutes, or until tomatoes begin to soften. Stir in mashed garlic, sun-dried tomatoes, and wine, and bring to a simmer.

3. Add cheese to wine by ½ cup measures, stirring constantly with a whisk in a figure-eight pattern. Add additional cheese only after the previous addition is melted.

4. Combine water and cornstarch in a small bowl, and stir to dissolve cornstarch. Add this mixture to fondue and bring to a simmer, stirring constantly. Cook over low heat for 1 to 2 minutes or until fondue has thickened. Season to taste with salt and pepper.

5. Transfer fondue to a fondue pot or other pot with a heat source, and serve with crusty bread cubes, steamed broccoli or cauliflower florets, steamed asparagus spears, cherry tomatoes, halved or quartered, steamed or oven-roasted new potatoes, or bite-size pieces of cooked chicken or baked ham.

Variation: A combination of Emmenthal and Gruyère or Gouda can be substituted for the cheddar.

Cheddar, Broccoli, and Roasted Red Pepper Fondue

| Serves: **6** | Prep time: **15 minutes** | Cook time: **25 minutes** |

1 (10-oz.) pkg. frozen chopped broccoli

1 cup dry white wine

½ cup dry vermouth

2 roasted red bell peppers, drained if from a jar, and finely chopped

1 TB. chopped fresh rosemary or 1 tsp. dried

1 lb. (4 cups) sharp cheddar cheese, coarsely grated

1 TB. cold water

1 TB. cornstarch

Salt and freshly ground black pepper to taste

1. Cook broccoli according to package directions. Drain well, pressing with the back of a spoon to extract as much liquid as possible. Place broccoli in a bowl, and mash it with a potato masher.

2. Place broccoli in a heavy 2-quart saucepan, and stir in wine, vermouth, roasted red peppers, and rosemary. Bring to a simmer over medium heat.

3. Add cheese to wine by ½ cup measures, stirring constantly with a whisk in a figure-eight pattern. Add additional cheese only after the previous addition is melted.

4. Combine water and cornstarch in a small bowl, and stir to dissolve cornstarch. Add to fondue, and bring to a simmer, stirring constantly. Cook over low heat for 1 to 2 minutes or until fondue has thickened. Season to taste with salt and pepper.

5. Transfer fondue to a fondue pot or other pot with a heat source, and serve with crusty French or Italian bread cubes, herbed foccacia, steamed broccoli or cauliflower florets, halved or quartered, steamed or oven-roasted new potatoes, cooked tortellini or gnocchi, or bite-size pieces of cooked chicken or roast pork.

Variation: Chopped asparagus or cauliflower can be used in place of the broccoli, and a combination of Emmenthal and Gruyère, jalapeño Jack, or Gouda can be substituted for the cheddar.

Brie, Stilton, and Wild Mushroom Fondue

| Serves: **6** | Prep time: **15 minutes** | Cook time: **25 minutes** |

1 garlic clove, peeled and halved crosswise

2 TB. dried porcini mushrooms, finely chopped

2 tsp. fresh thyme or ³/₄ tsp. dried

1¹/₂ cups dry white wine

2 TB. unsalted butter

2 TB. olive oil

¹/₄ lb. fresh shiitake mushrooms, stemmed and finely chopped

³/₄ lb. Brie cheese, at room temperature

¹/₄ lb. Stilton cheese, coarsely grated

1 TB. cold water

1 TB. cornstarch

Freshly ground black pepper to taste

1. Rub the inside of a heavy 2-quart saucepan with cut sides of garlic. Discard garlic. Add porcini mushrooms, thyme, and wine to the pan, and bring to a simmer over medium heat. Reduce heat to low, and simmer for 1 minute. Turn off heat, and allow mixture to *steep* for 10 minutes.

2. While mixture is steeping, heat butter and olive oil in a medium skillet over medium-high heat. When butter foam begins to subside, add chopped shiitake mushrooms. Cook, stirring constantly, for 3 minutes or until mushrooms are soft and browned. Add cooked mushrooms to the pan with wine.

3. Scrape the top rind off Brie, and scoop out interior cheese using a spoon. Discard bottom and side rinds.

4. Bring wine back to a simmer over medium heat. Add Brie and Stilton cheeses to wine by ¹/₂ cup measures, stirring constantly with a whisk in a figure-eight pattern. Add additional cheese only after the previous addition is melted.

5. Combine water and cornstarch in a small bowl, and stir to dissolve cornstarch. Add to fondue, and bring to a simmer, stirring constantly. Cook over low heat for 1 to 2 minutes or until fondue has thickened.

6. Transfer fondue to a fondue pot or other pot with a heat source, and serve with crusty French or Italian bread cubes, steamed broccoli or cauliflower florets, halved or quartered, steamed or oven-roasted new potatoes, cooked tortellini or ravioli, or bite-size pieces of cooked chicken or roast beef.

Variation: Camembert or Explorateur cheese can be substituted for the Brie, and Gorgonzola or blue cheese can be used in place of the Stilton.

nd Caramelized Shallot Fondue

Prep time: **15 minutes**	Cook time: **30 minutes**

3 TB. unsalted butter

1 TB. olive oil

½ lb. shallots, peeled and finely chopped

2 tsp. granulated sugar

Salt and freshly ground black pepper to taste

1 garlic clove, peeled and cut in half crosswise

1½ cups dry white wine

¾ lb. (3 cups) Gruyère cheese, coarsely grated

¼ lb. (1 cup) Emmenthal cheese, coarsely grated

1 TB. applejack brandy

1 TB. cornstarch

1. Melt butter and olive oil in a medium skillet over medium heat. Add shallots, toss to coat with butter mixture, and cover the pan. Cook for 5 minutes, uncover the pan, and sprinkle shallots with sugar, salt, and pepper. Increase the heat to medium-high, and cook shallots, stirring frequently, for 10 to 15 minutes or until shallots are browned. (You can do this up to 2 days ahead and refrigerate shallots, tightly covered with plastic wrap.)

2. Rub the inside of a heavy 2-quart saucepan with the cut sides of garlic. Discard garlic. Add wine and shallots to the pot, and bring to a simmer over medium heat.

3. Add Gruyère and Emmenthal cheeses to wine by ½ cup measures, stirring constantly with a whisk in a figure-eight pattern. Add additional cheese only after the previous addition is melted.

4. Combine applejack brandy and cornstarch in a small bowl, and stir to dissolve cornstarch. Add to fondue, and bring to a simmer, stirring constantly. Cook over low heat for 1 to 2 minutes or until fondue has thickened.

5. Transfer fondue to a fondue pot or other pot with a heat source, and serve with crusty French or Italian bread cubes, steamed broccoli or cauliflower florets, halved or quartered, steamed or oven-roasted new potatoes, cooked tortellini or ravioli, or bite-size pieces of cooked chicken or shrimp.

Variation: Cheddar cheese can be used in place of the Gruyère.

Swiss Cheese and Spinach Fondue

| Serves: **6** | Prep time: **15 minutes** | Cook time: **25 minutes** |

1 (10-oz.) pkg. frozen chopped spinach	1 lb. (4 cups) Emmenthal or Jarlsberg cheese, coarsely grated
1 cup half-and-half	1 TB. cold water
½ cup vegetable stock	1 TB. cornstarch
2 tsp. fresh thyme or ½ tsp. dried	Salt and freshly ground black pepper to taste
Pinch ground nutmeg	

1. Cook spinach according to package directions. Drain in a colander, pressing with the back of a spoon to extract as much liquid as possible.

2. Place spinach in a heavy 2-quart saucepan, and stir in half-and-half, vegetable stock, thyme, and nutmeg. Bring to a simmer over medium heat, stirring occasionally.

3. Add cheese to wine by ½ cup measures, stirring constantly with a whisk in a figure-eight pattern. Add additional cheese only after the previous addition is melted.

4. Combine water and cornstarch in a small bowl, and stir to dissolve cornstarch. Add to fondue, and bring to a simmer, stirring constantly. Cook over low heat for 1 to 2 minutes or until fondue has thickened, and season with salt and pepper.

5. Transfer fondue to a fondue pot or other pot with a heat source, and serve with crusty French or Italian bread cubes, steamed broccoli or cauliflower florets, halved or quartered, steamed or oven-roasted new potatoes, cooked gnocchi, or bite-size pieces of roast turkey or baked ham.

Variation: Cheddar cheese can be used in place of the Swiss cheese.

Fon-Don'ts

Vegetables with a high iron content like spinach or collard greens should never be cooked in an aluminum pot. The pot will give the vegetables a metallic taste

Three-Cheese, Carrot, and Chutney Fondue

| Serves: **6** | Prep time: **15 minutes** | Cook time: **25 minutes** |

½ cup mango chutney, such as Major Grey's

2 TB. unsalted butter

¼ lb. (1 cup) finely chopped carrot

1 tsp. granulated sugar

Salt and freshly ground black pepper to taste

½ lb. Brie, at room temperature

1 garlic clove, peeled and halved crosswise

1 cup dry white wine

½ cup sweet vermouth

½ lb. Emmenthal cheese, coarsely grated

¼ lb. Havarti cheese, coarsely grated

2 TB. kirsch

1 TB. cornstarch

1. Place chutney in a food processor fitted with a steel blade or in a blender, and chop finely using an on-and-off pulsing action. Set aside.

2. Melt butter in a small saucepan over medium heat. Add carrot, cover the pan, and reduce the heat to low. Cook carrot, stirring occasionally, for 5 to 10 minutes or until carrot is tender. Uncover the pan, raise the heat to medium, and sprinkle carrot with sugar, salt, and pepper. Cook 1 minute.

3. While carrot is cooking, scrape the top rind off Brie, and scoop out interior cheese using a spoon. Discard the bottom and side rinds.

4. Rub the inside of a heavy 2-quart saucepan with the cut sides of garlic. Discard garlic. Add wine, vermouth, carrot, and chutney to the pot, and bring to a simmer over medium heat.

5. Add Brie, Emmenthal, and Havarti cheeses to the wine by ½ cup measures, stirring constantly with a whisk in a figure-eight pattern. Add additional cheese only after the previous addition is melted.

6. Combine kirsch and cornstarch in a small bowl, and stir to dissolve cornstarch. Add to fondue and bring to a simmer, stirring constantly. Cook over low heat for 1 to 2 minutes or until fondue has thickened.

7. Transfer fondue to a fondue pot or other pot with a heat source. Serve with crusty French or Italian bread cubes, apple or pear slices, steamed broccoli or cauliflower florets, halved or quartered, steamed or oven-roasted new potatoes, or bite-size pieces of cooked chicken or shrimp.

Variation: Camembert or Explorateur can be used in place of the Brie, and Gruyère can be used instead of Emmenthal.

Brie and Pesto Fondue

| Serves: **6** | Prep time: **10 minutes** | Cook time: **10 minutes** |

$\frac{3}{4}$ lb. (3 cups) Brie cheese, softened

$1\frac{1}{2}$ cups dry white wine

$\frac{1}{3}$ cup refrigerated pesto sauce

$\frac{1}{2}$ lb. whole milk mozzarella cheese, cut into $\frac{1}{4}$-inch dice

1 TB. cold water

1 TB. cornstarch

Salt and freshly ground black pepper to taste

1. Scrape the top rind off Brie, and scoop out the interior cheese using a spoon. Discard the bottom and side rinds. Set aside.

2. Combine wine and pesto sauce in a heavy 2-quart saucepan and whisk well. Bring to a simmer over medium heat.

3. Add Brie and mozzarella cheeses to wine by $\frac{1}{2}$ cup measures, stirring constantly with a whisk in a figure-eight pattern. Add additional cheese only after the previous addition is melted.

4. Combine water and cornstarch in a small bowl, and stir to dissolve cornstarch. Add to fondue and bring to a simmer, stirring constantly. Cook over low heat for 1 to 2 minutes or until fondue has thickened.

5. Transfer fondue to a fondue pot or other pot with a heat source, and serve with crusty French or Italian bread cubes, steamed broccoli or cauliflower florets, halved or quartered, steamed or oven-roasted new potatoes, cooked tortellini or ravioli, or bite-size pieces of cooked chicken or baked ham.

Variation: Camembert or Explorateur cheese can be used instead of Brie.

Fondue Facts

Pesto means "pounded" in Italian, and forms of this garlicky sauce can be traced back to the Romans. We currently associate it with Liguria in general and Genoa in particular, but the first recipe for our contemporary version appears in a cookbook from Florence in 1848.

Gorgonzola, Pear, and Walnut Fonduta

| Serves: **6** | Prep time: **20 minutes** | Cook time: **15 minutes** |

½ cup finely chopped walnuts

3 TB. unsalted butter

2 ripe pears, peeled, cored, and finely chopped

2 tsp. granulated sugar

1½ cups whole milk

½ lb. (2 cups) Gorgonzola cheese, coarsely grated

½ lb. (2 cups) whole milk mozzarella cheese, cut into ¼-inch cubes

4 large egg yolks

¼ cup heavy cream

1. Toast walnuts in a 350°F oven for 5 to 7 minutes, or until brown. Set aside.

2. Melt butter in a skillet over medium heat. Add pears and sprinkle with sugar. Cook, stirring occasionally, for 3 to 5 minutes, or until pears are soft. Add milk to the skillet, raise the heat to medium, and bring to a simmer, stirring occasionally.

3. Transfer pear mixture to the top of a double boiler set over simmering water, and stir in toasted walnuts. Add Gorgonzola and mozzarella cheeses to fondue by ½ cup measures, stirring constantly with a whisk in a figure-eight pattern. Add additional cheese only after the previous addition is melted.

4. Whisk egg yolks with cream in a mixing bowl. Slowly whisk 1 cup of mixture from the double boiler into egg yolks and then pour egg mixture into the double boiler. Reduce heat to low and cook, stirring constantly, until mixture thickens and coats the back of a spoon. Do not let mixture boil.

5. Transfer fondue to a fondue pot or other pot with a heat source, and serve with pear or apple slices, crusty French or Italian bread cubes, steamed broccoli or cauliflower florets, steamed asparagus spears, cooked gnocchi, or bite-size pieces of cooked chicken or shrimp.

Variation: Any blue-veined cheese, such as blue cheese or Stilton, can be used in place of the Gorgonzola.

Mozzarella, Herb, and Olive Fonduta

| Serves: **6** | Prep time: **10 minutes** | Cook time: **15 minutes** |

1½ cups whole milk

2 TB. chopped fresh oregano or 2 tsp. dried

2 TB. chopped fresh basil or 2 tsp. dried

1 TB. fresh thyme or 1 tsp. dried

1 cup pitted kalamata olives, finely chopped

1 lb. (4 cups) whole milk mozzarella cheese, cut into ¼-inch cubes

4 large egg yolks

¼ cup heavy cream

Salt and freshly ground black pepper to taste

1. Combine milk, oregano, basil, thyme, and olives in the top of a double boiler set over simmering water, and allow milk to come to a simmer.

2. Add mozzarella cheese to milk by ½ cup measures, stirring constantly with a whisk in a figure-eight pattern. Add additional cheese only after the previous addition is melted.

3. Whisk egg yolks with cream in a mixing bowl. Slowly whisk 1 cup of mixture from the double boiler into egg yolks and then pour egg mixture into the double boiler. Reduce the heat to low and cook, stirring constantly, until mixture thickens and coats the back of a spoon. Do not let mixture boil. Season to taste with salt and pepper.

4. Transfer fondue to a fondue pot or other pot with a heat source, and serve with crusty French or Italian bread cubes, fresh fennel wedges, fresh mushrooms, steamed broccoli or cauliflower florets, cooked tortellini or ravioli, or bite-size pieces of cooked chicken or pepperoni.

Variation: Any type of chopped olive can be used in place of the kalamata olives, and capers can be substitute for olives

Dip Tips

If you don't have a double boiler, you can improvise one. Find a mixing bowl that fits into a saucepan. It doesn't have to fit perfectly as long as the rounded bottom extends into the pan. Then fill the pan with water up to the bottom of the bowl and bring it to a boil.

Chapter 5

Melts with More

In This Chapter

◆ Meaty and seafood-y fondues

◆ Spicy fondues with international flair

◆ Fondues with a classic white sauce base

Pairing meats with cheeses is a natural combination (just think about a cheeseburger or a pizza topped with succulent sausage), and that extends to pairing these two protein packed foods in a fondue. That's the theme for the recipes in this chapter, and there's a great deal of variety within the two categories of starring ingredients.

In the previous two chapters, the fondues have all been thickened with cornstarch. In this chapter, you'll find some recipes that use a basic white sauce as the foundation for the fondue. If you've ever made a cream sauce or a cheese sauce, you already know how to do it. And if you haven't, you'll be able to transfer the skills you learn from making these recipes to general cooking.

The Benefits of Browning

Browning the meats is an all-important step to the success of these recipes. It traps the natural juices and flavor in the meat while adding a rich color to both the meat and the sauce. It also forces fat within the meat to the surface, which can then be removed to reduce the fat content of the meal. It also keeps the meat from forming a large clump in the middle of your saucepan.

Meat should be browned in a skillet rather than in a saucepan. It needs room to be stirred, and the high sides of a saucepan tend to create meat that's steamed in its own juices rather than browned. Plus, part of the browning process is to break up the meat into tiny parts. It's worth it to wash the extra pot and brown the meat separately.

Smoked Cheddar, Tomato, and Bacon Fondue

| Serves: **6** | Prep time: **15 minutes** | Cook time: **25 minutes** |

$\frac{1}{2}$ lb. bacon, cut into $\frac{1}{4}$-inch slices

2 plum tomatoes, cored, seeded, and finely chopped

1 cup dry white wine

$\frac{1}{2}$ cup tomato juice

2 TB. chopped fresh parsley

1 TB. Dijon mustard

2 tsp. fresh thyme or $\frac{1}{2}$ tsp. dried

1 lb. (4 cups) smoked cheddar cheese, coarsely grated

1 TB. cold water

1 TB. cornstarch

Salt and freshly ground black pepper to taste

1. Place bacon in a heavy 2-quart saucepan over medium-high heat. Cook, stirring occasionally, for 7 to 10 minutes or until crisp. Remove bacon from the pan with a slotted spoon, and set aside.

2. Pour all but 1 tablespoon bacon fat from the pan. Add tomatoes and cook for 2 minutes or until tomatoes begin to soften. Add wine, tomato juice, parsley, Dijon mustard, and thyme to the pan, and bring to a simmer.

3. Add cheddar cheese to wine by $\frac{1}{2}$ cup measures, stirring constantly with a whisk in a figure-eight pattern. Add additional cheese only after the previous addition is melted.

4. Combine water and cornstarch in a small bowl, and stir to dissolve cornstarch. Add to fondue and bring to a simmer, stirring constantly. Cook over low heat for 1 to 2 minutes or until fondue has thickened. Season to taste with salt and pepper.

5. Transfer fondue to a fondue pot or other pot with a heat source, and serve with crusty French or Italian bread cubes, cherry tomatoes, steamed broccoli or cauliflower florets, halved or quartered, steamed or oven-roasted new potatoes, or cooked gnocchi or tortellini.

Dip Tips

Substituting some of the precooked bacon products on the market for the raw bacon will definitely shortcut both the preparation and cooking time for this dish. Just be sure the product is actually precooked bacon, not a synthetic, bacon-flavored product.

Variation: Finely chopped ham or browned and cooked sausage can be substituted for the bacon.

Cheddar, Vegetable, and Ham Fondue

| Serves: **6** | Prep time: **15 minutes** | Cook time: **15 minutes** |

2 TB. unsalted butter

1/2 lb. cooked ham, trimmed of all fat and finely chopped

1 small onion, peeled and finely chopped

1/2 green or red bell pepper, seeds and ribs removed, and finely chopped

2 garlic cloves, peeled and minced

1 (12-oz.) can lager beer

1 lb. (4 cups) sharp cheddar cheese, coarsely grated

1 TB. cold water

1 TB. cornstarch

Salt and freshly ground black pepper to taste

1. Heat butter in a skillet over medium heat. Add ham, onion, bell pepper, and garlic. Cook, stirring frequently, for 5 to 7 minutes or until vegetables are soft.

2. Scrape mixture into a heavy 2-quart saucepan and add beer. Bring to a simmer over medium-high heat.

3. Add cheddar cheese to beer by 1/2 cup measures, stirring constantly with a whisk in a figure-eight pattern. Add additional cheese only after the previous addition is melted.

4. Combine water and cornstarch in a small bowl, and stir to dissolve cornstarch. Add to fondue, and bring to a simmer, stirring constantly. Cook over low heat for 1 to 2 minutes or until fondue has thickened. Season to taste with salt and pepper.

5. Transfer fondue to a fondue pot or other pot with a heat source, and serve with crusty French or Italian bread cubes, fresh fennel wedges, steamed broccoli or cauliflower florets, halved or quartered, steamed or oven-roasted new potatoes, or cooked tortellini or ravioli.

Variations: Chorizo sausage and jalapeño Jack cheese can be used to give this recipe a Mexican taste.

Feta, Chevre and Lamb Fondue

| Serves: **6** | Prep time: **15 minutes** | Cook time: **25 minutes** |

1 TB. olive oil

$^{1}/_{2}$ lb. lean ground lamb

1 small onion, peeled and finely chopped

3 garlic cloves, peeled and minced

1 cup dry white wine

$^{1}/_{2}$ cup tomato juice

2 TB. chopped fresh oregano or 2 tsp. dried

2 TB. chopped fresh dill or 2 tsp. dried

$^{1}/_{2}$ lb. (2 cups) whole milk mozzarella cheese, cut into $^{1}/_{4}$-inch cubes

$^{1}/_{4}$ lb. (1 cup) feta cheese, crumbled

$^{1}/_{4}$ lb. (1 cup) chevre or other goat cheese, crumbled

1 TB. cold water

1 TB. cornstarch

Salt and freshly ground black pepper to taste

1. Heat olive oil in a skillet over medium-high heat. Add lamb and cook, breaking up lumps with a fork, 5 to 7 minutes or until lamb is brown. Remove lamb from the skillet with a slotted spoon and place it in a heavy 2-quart saucepan.

2. Discard all but 1 tablespoon fat from skillet, and add onion and garlic. Cook, stirring frequently, for 5 to 7 minutes or until onion is soft. Scrape mixture into the saucepan, and add wine, tomato juice, oregano, and dill. Bring to a simmer over medium heat.

3. Add mozzarella, feta, and goat cheeses to wine by $^{1}/_{2}$ cup measures, stirring constantly with a whisk in a figure-eight pattern. Add additional cheese only after the previous addition is melted.

4. Combine water and cornstarch in a small bowl, and stir to dissolve cornstarch. Add to fondue and bring to a simmer, stirring constantly. Cook over low heat for 1 to 2 minutes or until fondue has thickened. Season to taste with salt and pepper.

5. Transfer fondue to a fondue pot or other pot with a heat source, and serve with crusty French or Italian bread cubes, pita bread squares, cherry tomatoes, fennel wedges, steamed broccoli or cauliflower florets, halved or quartered, steamed or oven-roasted new potatoes, or cooked gnocchi.

Pizza Fondue with Italian Sausage

| Serves: **6** | Prep time: **10 minutes** | Cook time: **20 minutes** |

1 TB. olive oil
½ lb. sweet or hot Italian bulk sausage
1 medium onion, peeled and finely chopped
3 garlic cloves, peeled and minced
1½ cups dry white wine
2 tsp. Italian seasoning

¾ lb. (3 cups) whole milk mozzarella cheese, cut into ¼-inch dice
¼ lb. fontina cheese, coarsely grated
2 TB. freshly grated Parmesan cheese
1 TB. cold water
1 TB. cornstarch
Salt and red pepper flakes to taste

1. Heat olive oil in a medium skillet over medium-high heat. Add sausage, breaking up any lumps with a fork. Cook, stirring frequently, 5 to 7 minutes or until sausage is brown. Remove sausage from the skillet with a slotted spoon and place it in a heavy 2-quart saucepan.

2. Discard all but 2 tablespoons fat from the skillet, and return the pan to medium heat. Add onion and garlic, and cook, stirring frequently, for 5 to 7 minutes or until onion is soft. Add mixture to the saucepan, and stir in wine and Italian seasoning. Bring to a simmer over medium heat, stirring occasionally.

3. Add mozzarella, fontina, and Parmesan cheeses to wine by ½ cup measures, stirring constantly with a whisk in a figure-eight pattern. Add additional cheese only after the previous addition is melted.

4. Combine water and cornstarch in a small bowl, and stir to dissolve cornstarch. Add to fondue and bring to a simmer, stirring constantly. Cook over low heat for 1 to 2 minutes or until fondue has thickened. Season with salt and red pepper flakes.

5. Transfer fondue to a fondue pot or other pot with a heat source, and serve with crusty French or Italian bread cubes, steamed broccoli or cauliflower florets, halved or quartered, steamed or oven-roasted new potatoes, cooked tortellini or ravioli, or bite-size pieces of cooked chicken or baked ham.

Chipotle Cheese and Chorizo Fondue

| Serves: **6** | Prep time: **10 minutes** | Cook time: **20 minutes** |

1 TB. olive oil

$\frac{1}{2}$ lb. bulk chorizo sausage

1 TB. unsalted butter

1 small onion, peeled and finely chopped

4 garlic cloves, peeled and minced

1 cup heavy cream

1 (4-oz.) can chopped mild green chilies, drained

3 canned chipotle chilies in adobo sauce, finely chopped

$\frac{1}{2}$ lb. (2 cups) Monterey Jack cheese, coarsely grated

$\frac{1}{2}$ lb. (2 cups) mild cheddar cheese, coarsely grated

2 TB. tequila

1 TB. cornstarch

Salt and cayenne to taste

1. Heat olive oil in a skillet over medium-high heat. Add chorizo and cook, breaking up lumps with a fork, 5 to 7 minutes or until chorizo is brown. Remove chorizo from the skillet with a slotted spoon and place it in a heavy 2-quart saucepan.

2. Discard grease from the skillet, reduce heat to medium, and add butter. Add onion and garlic and cook, stirring frequently, 5 to 7 minutes or until onion is soft. Scrape mixture into the saucepan, and add cream, green chilies, and chipotle chilies. Bring to a simmer, stirring occasionally.

3. Add Monterey Jack and cheddar cheeses to cream by $\frac{1}{2}$ cup measures, stirring constantly with a whisk in a figure-eight pattern. Add additional cheese only after the previous addition is melted.

4. Combine tequila and cornstarch in a small bowl, and stir to dissolve cornstarch. Add to fondue and bring to a simmer, stirring constantly. Cook over low heat for 1 to 2 minutes or until fondue has thickened. Season to taste with salt and cayenne.

Fon-Don'ts

When dealing with chipotles in adobo sauce, be sure to scrape off all the sauce from the chilies before chopping them. Otherwise, you'll get even more fiery flavor. But don't rinse them. That diminishes the smoky nuances.

5. Transfer fondue to a fondue pot or other pot with a heat source, and serve with crusty French or Italian bread cubes, flour or corn tortilla squares, cherry tomatoes, jicama slices, steamed broccoli or cauliflower florets, or halved or quartered, steamed or oven-roasted new potatoes.

Swiss Cheese and Crab Fondue

| Serves: **6** | Prep time: **15 minutes** | Cook time: **25 minutes** |

3 TB. unsalted butter

4 scallions, trimmed with all but 2 inches of green tops discarded, and finely chopped

$^1\!/_4$ green or red bell pepper, seeds and ribs removed, and finely chopped

$^1\!/_2$ celery rib, finely chopped

3 TB. all-purpose flour

1 TB. *Old Bay* seasoning or to taste

$1^1\!/_4$ cups heavy cream

$^1\!/_4$ cup dry white wine

1 TB. freshly squeezed lemon juice

1 lb. (4 cups) Emmenthal cheese, coarsely grated

$^1\!/_2$ lb. crabmeat, picked over to remove shell fragments

Salt and freshly ground black pepper to taste

1. Melt butter in a heavy 2-quart saucepan over medium heat. Add scallions, bell pepper, and celery, and cook, stirring frequently, 5 to 7 minutes or until vegetables are soft. Reduce heat to low, add flour, and cook 2 minutes, stirring constantly. Add Old Bay Seasoning, and stir to blend.

2. Raise the heat to medium, and whisk in cream, wine, and lemon juice. Bring to a boil, whisking until smooth.

3. Add Emmenthal cheese to sauce by $^1\!/_2$ cup measures, stirring constantly with a whisk in a figure-eight pattern. Add additional cheese only after the previous addition is melted. Stir in crab, and season to taste with salt and pepper.

4. Transfer fondue to a fondue pot or other pot with a heat source, and serve with crusty French or Italian bread cubes, steamed broccoli or cauliflower florets, halved or quartered, steamed or oven-roasted new potatoes, cooked tortellini or ravioli, or bite-size pieces of cooked chicken or baked ham.

Variations: Chopped lobster or shrimp can be used in place of the crabmeat.

Dip-Tionary

Old Bay is a seasoning mix developed for the Chesapeake Bay's prized steamed crabs. It contains celery salt, mustard, cayenne, bay leaves, cloves, allspice, ginger, and paprika.

Sherried Cheddar and Shrimp Fondue (Shrimp Newburg)

| Serves: **6** | Prep time: **15 minutes** | Cook time: **15 minutes** |

3 TB. unsalted butter

4 scallions, trimmed with all but 2 inches of green tops discarded, and finely chopped

3 TB. all-purpose flour

1 TB. sweet paprika

1 TB. tomato paste

1 cup heavy cream

$\frac{1}{2}$ cup dry sherry

1 TB. freshly squeezed lemon juice

1 lb. (4 cups) mild cheddar cheese, coarsely grated

$\frac{1}{2}$ lb. cooked salad shrimp (more than 45 per lb.), finely chopped

Salt and cayenne to taste

1. Melt butter in a heavy 2-quart saucepan over medium heat. Add scallions and cook, stirring constantly, 3 minutes or until scallions are soft. Reduce heat to low, add flour, and cook 2 minutes, stirring constantly. Add paprika and tomato paste, and stir to blend.

2. Raise heat to medium and whisk in cream, sherry, and lemon juice. Bring to a boil, whisking until smooth.

3. Add cheese to sauce by $\frac{1}{2}$ cup measures, stirring constantly with a whisk in a figure-eight pattern. Add additional cheese only after the previous addition is melted.

4. Stir in shrimp and season to taste with salt and cayenne.

Fondue Facts

This fondue has the same basic flavors as Shrimp Newburg, which was developed at the famed Delmonico's restaurant in New York in the mid-nineteenth century. There it was served over toast points to the after-theater crowd.

5. Transfer fondue to a fondue pot or other pot with a heat source, and serve with crusty French or Italian bread cubes, steamed broccoli or cauliflower florets, halved or quartered, steamed or oven-roasted new potatoes, cooked tortellini or ravioli, or bite-size pieces of cooked chicken or baked ham.

Curried Monterey Jack and Chicken Fondue

Serves: 6 | **Prep time: 10 minutes** | **Cook time: 20 minutes**

3 TB. unsalted butter

2 shallots, peeled and finely chopped

3 TB. all-purpose flour

2 to 3 TB. curry powder or to taste

1¼ cups heavy cream

¼ cup sweet vermouth

1 TB. freshly squeezed lemon juice

1 lb. (4 cups) Monterey Jack cheese, coarsely grated

½ lb. cooked chicken, finely chopped

¼ cup chutney, finely chopped

Salt and freshly ground black pepper to taste

1. Melt butter in a heavy 2-quart saucepan over medium heat. Add shallots, and cook, stirring constantly, 3 minutes or until shallots are soft. Reduce heat to low, add flour and curry powder, and cook 2 minutes, stirring constantly.

2. Raise heat to medium, and whisk in cream, vermouth, and lemon juice. Bring to a boil, whisking until smooth.

3. Add Monterey Jack cheese to sauce by ½ cup measures, stirring constantly with a whisk in a figure-eight pattern. Add additional cheese only after the previous addition is melted.

4. Stir in chicken and chutney, and season to taste with salt and pepper.

5. Transfer fondue to a fondue pot or other pot with a heat source, and serve with crusty French or Italian bread cubes, hard-boiled egg wedges, cherry tomatoes, steamed broccoli or cauliflower florets, or halved or quartered, steamed or oven-roasted new potatoes.

Dip Tips

Spice blends like curry powder and chili powder are added before the liquid so the spices will toast and lose any harsh or raw taste.

Part 3

Tabletop Cooking

Up to this point in the book, everything has arrived at the table ready to eat. But that's not true for the dishes in Part 3. Here I detail recipes intended to be cooked by diners right before eating them, with or without dipping them into some sort of sauce.

The focus of Chapter 6 is fondues cooked in hot oil. Some of these foods are marinated before cooking for additional zing. Chapter 7 turns the table. The foods there are plain, and it's the cooking mediums—infused broths—that add complexity to the dishes.

Important to both oil- and broth-cooked fondues are simple sauces in which you can dip the food after it emerges from the pot. Find the easy recipes for these in Chapter 8.

Chapter 6

Fried with Flair

In This Chapter

♦ Classic meat fondue

♦ International meat and fish fondues

♦ Vegetarian fondues

All the recipes in this chapter are for dishes that are fried in hot oil at the table, but that's where the similarity ends. The ingredients range from lean meats to healthful vegetables, and the oil itself can be plain or flavored with other ingredients. Sometimes the foods are marinated before cooking; other times they're not.

Many of these recipes are related to classic *Fondue Bourguignonne*, which gained popularity along with cheese fondue in the 1970s. The meat is plain, but it's then dipped in any number of sauces (you'll find the sauce recipes in Chapter 8).

Fried fondues are great for quick meals. In no time, the oil can be heated and you're ready to serve.

Fundamentals of Frying

Frying, like boiling, is a cooking method that uses a liquid medium to transfer heat to food to cook it. But boiling water is 212°F, while the oil used for frying foods can be heated to twice that temperature. That's what gives fried foods their crispy exterior. The heat of the fat seals the surface and keeps the interior of the food moist.

Frying is easy to do well, and it's not messy if you follow certain procedures. And frying is fast, which you and your guests are sure to appreciate.

Fear of Frying

You can use a basic vegetable oil when frying for these recipes. Or you can use peanut oil, corn oil, canola oil, or a blend. I've listed vegetable oil for these recipes, but any bland oil is fine.

Use as much oil for frying to fill your fondue pot halfway full. If it's any fuller than that, you risk the oil splashing out when food is added. However, you don't want to skimp on the oil, either. The oil level must be high enough that the food is covered with the oil and so it maintains the proper temperature when cold food is added.

Fon-Don'ts

Don't use olive oil or butter to fry. The finer the olive oil, the more impurities it contains from olives, and these burn at a high temperature. The same holds true for the dairy solids in butter. "All vegetable" shortening options don't contain impurities, but they do contain high amounts of synthetic trans fats which have been identified as the worst type of fat for your heart health. So ban shortening from the list of options as well.

Taking the Temperature

Foods for fondue should be fried at 375°F. If the oil is too cool, you get pale, greasy food. If oil is too hot, you get food that's burned on the outside before the inside is cooked.

The best way to test the oil temperature is with a deep-frying thermometer. Be sure it's submerged in the center of the oil, rather than resting on the bottom of the pot, where the reading will be inflated from the heat of the pot.

If you don't have a deep-frying thermometer, you can judge the oil's temperature visually. Drop a cube of bread into the hot oil. If a ring of white bubbles surrounds the bread and the bread turns golden brown in about 15 seconds, the oil is hot enough.

Culling the Cuts

Size and quality are the two important factors when assembling food for an oil fondue. The recipes in this chapter are not ones that use bargain cuts; save those for slowly braised stews. For meat fondues, use lean meat that doesn't contain a lot of connective tissue, which gets very tough when cooked quickly.

Meat counters today contain a dizzying number of cuts. And you want lean cuts for fondue, which are the most expensive. Here are some general guidelines for selecting cuts of meat:

◆ Beef should be either tenderloin or very lean sirloin, and all visible fat should be removed. Flank steak is lean, but it should only be used if it's thinly sliced on the diagonal rather than cubed.

◆ Pork tenderloin and center of the loin are the best choices. The fat and gristle should be trimmed on both.

◆ Leg of lamb, trimmed of all fat, is an excellent and moderately priced choice for rich meat. An alternative is the eye of rib taken from a rack of lamb; however, it will cost far more money.

◆ Veal is tender by nature, and almost any cut will do. Just be sure it's been trimmed of fat.

Eating Etiquette

Fondues cooked in oil have a variation on the etiquette pointers I discussed in Chapter 1. You still shouldn't eat food directly from the fork placed in the fondue pot. But germs aren't the only reason; the fork will be extremely hot after being submerged in the oil.

When serving, give diners two fondue forks to supplement the table fork and knife. Using this system, foods such as chicken cubes that require a long cooking time can be cooked alongside fast-cooking foods like vegetables or shrimp. It's up to each individual diner to keep track of what they have cooking in the pot and when it should be removed.

Guests also appreciate if half their plates are lined with paper napkins to absorb grease. They can blot food on the napkins and then transfer it to the other side of the plate for cutting and dipping.

French Meat Fondue
(*Fondue Bourguignonne*)

Serves: 6   **Prep time: 15 minutes**

1½ lb. beef fillet, trimmed of all visible fat and cut into 1-inch cubes

Salt and freshly ground black pepper to taste

2 cups vegetable oil for frying, plus more as necessary

Suggested sauces: Blue Cheese Sauce, Louis Sauce, Herbed Tomato Sauce (recipes in Chapter 8)

1. Arrange beef cubes on a platter and season to taste with salt and pepper.

2. Heat oil in a saucepan over medium heat until it reaches 375°F. Transfer oil to a metal fondue pot or other metal pot with a heat source. Cook beef for 2 to 3 minutes or to desired doneness. Serve with desired sauce(s).

Variation: You can substitute cubes of pork, lamb, veal, or chicken for the beef, and any of the sauces in Chapter 8 can be substituted for those listed here.

Dip Tips

Classic beef fondue should be served with at least three sauces that have different flavor profiles. European sauces are traditional, but you can use Asian or Hispanic sauces as well.

Middle Eastern Herbed Lamb Meatball Fondue

Serves: 6   **Prep time: 25 minutes**

½ cup pine nuts

2 TB. olive oil

1 small onion, peeled and finely chopped

3 garlic cloves, peeled and minced

2 large eggs, lightly beaten

½ cup plain breadcrumbs

¼ cup milk

3 TB. chopped fresh parsley

2 TB. chopped fresh oregano or 2 tsp. dried

2 tsp. ground cumin

2 tsp. ground coriander

1½ lb. lean ground lamb

Salt and freshly ground black pepper to taste

2 cups vegetable oil for frying, plus more as necessary

Suggested sauces: Cucumber Raita, Herbed Tomato Sauce, Tahini Sauce (recipes in Chapter 8)

1. Place a medium skillet over medium heat. Add pine nuts and toast, shaking the pan occasionally, 3 to 5 minutes or until nuts are lightly browned. Remove nuts from the pan with a slotted spoon, and place them in a mixing bowl.

2. Add olive oil, onion, and garlic to the skillet. Cook, stirring frequently, 3 minutes or until onion is translucent. Scrape mixture into the mixing bowl, and add eggs, breadcrumbs, milk, parsley, oregano, cumin, coriander, and lamb. Mix well, and season to taste with salt and pepper.

3. Form mixture into 1-inch balls, and arrange on a platter. (You can do this up to 6 hours in advance and refrigerate, tightly covered with plastic wrap.)

4. Heat vegetable oil in a saucepan over medium heat until it reaches 375°F. Transfer oil to a metal fondue pot or other metal pot with a heat source. Cook meatballs 3 to 4 minutes or to desired doneness. Serve with desired sauce(s).

Variation: Place a ½ inch cube feta cheese in the center of each meatball, or add ½ cup chopped pitted kalamata olives to the meat mixture.

Indonesian Mixed Satay Fondue

Serves: 6 | *Prep time:* **20 minutes plus 2 hours for marinating**

$\frac{1}{2}$ cup soy sauce

$\frac{1}{2}$ cup firmly packed dark brown sugar

$\frac{1}{4}$ cup freshly squeezed lime juice

2 TB. Chinese chili sauce, or hot red pepper sauce to taste

2 TB. Asian sesame oil

4 garlic cloves, peeled and minced

2 TB. chopped fresh cilantro

$\frac{1}{2}$ lb. boneless, skinless chicken breasts, rinsed and patted dry

with paper towels, cut into 1-inch cubes

$\frac{1}{2}$ lb. pork tenderloin, trimmed of all fat and *silver skin*, and cut into 1-inch cubes

$\frac{1}{2}$ lb. extra large (16 to 20 count) raw shrimp, peeled and deveined

2 cups vegetable oil for frying, plus more as necessary

Suggested sauces: Spicy Thai Peanut Sauce, Ponzu Sauce, Uncooked Asian Dipping Sauce (recipes in Chapter 8)

1. Combine soy sauce, brown sugar, lime juice, Chinese chili sauce, Asian sesame oil, garlic, and cilantro in a mixing bowl. Whisk well to dissolve sugar. Transfer marinade to a heavy resealable plastic bag, and add chicken, pork, and shrimp. Refrigerate for 2 to 4 hours, turning the bag occasionally.

2. Remove food from marinade, and discard marinade. Pat food dry with a paper towel, and arrange it on a serving platter. (You can do this up to 6 hours in advance and refrigerate it, tightly covered with plastic wrap.)

3. Heat vegetable oil in a saucepan over medium heat until it reaches 375°F. Transfer oil to a metal fondue pot or other metal pot with a heat source. Cook chicken 4 to 5 minutes or until cooked through and no longer pink. Cook pork and shrimp 2 to 3 minutes or to desired doneness. Serve with desired sauce(s).

Variation: You can substitute cubes of beef, firm-fleshed fish fillets like swordfish, or vegetables such as scallions for the ingredients suggested here.

Dip-Tionary

Silver skin is the thin, almost iridescent coating on lean cuts of meat like tenderloins. It's thin but it's tough and must be trimmed away so the meat doesn't curl when it's cooked.

Sea Scallop and Shrimp Fondue with Sesame Orange Dipping Sauce

| *Serves:* **6** | *Prep time:* **20 minutes plus 1 hour for marinating** |

¼ cup sesame seeds

½ cup honey

½ cup rice wine vinegar

4 garlic cloves, peeled and minced

3 TB. grated fresh ginger

2 TB. soy sauce

2 TB. Asian sesame oil

1 TB. Asian chili sauce, or hot red pepper sauce to taste

1 TB. grated orange zest

¾ lb. sea scallops, rinsed and halved if large

1 lb. extra large (16 to 20 count) raw shrimp, peeled and deveined

13 scallions, 12 trimmed with all but 2 inches of green tops discarded and 1 trimmed and finely chopped

1 red bell pepper, seeds and ribs removed, and cut into 1-inch squares

½ lb. white mushrooms, wiped clean with a damp paper towel, trimmed and halved if large

2 cups vegetable oil for frying, plus more as necessary

2 TB. chopped fresh cilantro

1. Toast sesame seeds in a dry skillet over medium heat until lightly browned. Set aside.

2. Combine honey, rice wine vinegar, garlic, ginger, soy sauce, Asian sesame oil, Asian chili sauce, and orange zest in a mixing bowl. Whisk well. Add scallops and shrimp, and marinate, refrigerate for 1 hour, tightly covered.

3. Remove seafood from marinade with a slotted spoon, and pat dry with paper towels. Arrange on a platter with 12 trimmed scallions, red bell pepper, and mushrooms. (You can do this up to 6 hours in advance and refrigerate, tightly covered with plastic wrap.)

4. Heat vegetable oil in a saucepan over medium heat to 375°F. While oil is heating, stir sesame seeds, cilantro, and chopped scallions into marinade, and transfer marinade to a serving bowl.

5. Transfer oil to a metal fondue pot or another metal pot with a heat source. To serve, fry seafood and vegetables in hot oil for 1½ to 2 minutes or to desired doneness. Dip cooked food into bowls of reserved marinade.

Spicy Asian Chicken Fondue

| Serves: **6** | Prep time: **15 minutes plus 2 hours for marinating** |

2 large eggs

8 garlic cloves, peeled and minced

3 TB. soy sauce

2 TB. Asian sesame oil

1 tsp. plus 2 TB. ground ginger

$\frac{1}{2}$ tsp. plus 1 TB. Chinese five-spice powder

Freshly ground black pepper to taste

$1\frac{1}{2}$ lb. boneless, skinless chicken breasts, rinsed and patted dry with paper towels, cut into 1-inch cubes

1 cup all-purpose flour

2 cups vegetable oil for frying, plus more as necessary

$\frac{1}{4}$ cup finely chopped fresh ginger

2 small dried Chinese chilies

Suggested sauces: Ponzu Sauce, Indonesian Barbecue Sauce, Sesame Honey Mustard Sauce (recipes in Chapter 8)

1. Combine eggs, 2 garlic cloves, soy sauce, Asian sesame oil, 1 teaspoon ground ginger, $\frac{1}{2}$ teaspoon Chinese five-spice powder, and pepper in a mixing bowl. Whisk well, stir in chicken cubes, and refrigerate, tightly covered with plastic wrap, 2 hours.

2. Combine flour, remaining 2 tablespoons ground ginger, and remaining 1 tablespoon Chinese five-spice powder in a heavy plastic bag. Remove chicken from marinade with a slotted spoon, and toss it, a few pieces at a time, in seasoned flour. Arrange chicken cubes on a platter. (This can be done up to 4 hours in advance and refrigerated, tightly covered with plastic wrap.)

3. Combine vegetable oil, remaining 6 garlic cloves, chopped fresh ginger, and Chinese chilies in a saucepan. Heat over medium heat to 375°F. Skim off and discard garlic, ginger, and chilies.

4. Transfer oil to a metal fondue pot or another metal pot with a heat source. To serve, fry chicken cubes 4 to 5 minutes or until crisp, cooked through, and no longer pink. Serve with desired sauce(s).

Variation: Cubes of pork tenderloin or beef can be substituted for the chicken.

Spicy Southwestern Mixed-Meat Fondue

| *Serves:* **6** | *Prep time:* **15 minutes plus 2 hours for marinating** |

⅓ cup balsamic vinegar

4 garlic cloves, peeled and minced

3 TB. chili powder

1 TB. dried oregano, preferably Mexican

2 tsp. ground cumin

Salt and freshly ground black pepper to taste

1 lb. lean beef, cut into 1-inch cubes

1 lb. boneless turkey breast, rinsed and patted dry with paper towels, cut into 1-inch cubes

2 cups vegetable oil for frying, plus more as necessary

Suggested sauces: Uncooked Salsa Sauce, Creamy Chipotle Sauce, Mexican Tomato Sauce (recipes in Chapter 8)

1. Combine balsamic vinegar, garlic, chili powder, oregano, cumin, salt, and pepper in a stainless-steel or glass bowl. Whisk well, and add beef and turkey cubes. Refrigerate meats, covered with plastic wrap, at least 2 hours. Remove meat from marinade, and discard marinade. Pat meats dry with a paper towel.

2. Heat vegetable oil in a saucepan over medium heat until it reaches 375°F. Transfer oil to a metal fondue pot or other metal pot with a heat source. Cook beef 2 to 3 minutes or to desired doneness. Cook turkey 4 to 5 minutes or until cooked through and no longer pink. Serve with desired sauce(s).

Variation: You can substitute cubes of chicken breast, pork tenderloin, or leg of lamb. If you use extra-large shrimp or cubes of fish, reduce the marinating time for these foods to 1 hour.

Dip Tips

When serving an oil-cooked fondue, be sure to tie your accompanying vegetables to the theme of the dish. For example, for this recipe, crunchy jicama spears, tomato wedges, avocado slices are good choices, and they can be flavored with the same sauces used for dipping.

Italian Vegetable Fondue with Anchovy-Garlic Oil (*Bagna Cauda*)

Serves: 6   **Prep time: 25 minutes**

1 head broccoli, broken into florets

¼ lb. asparagus, trimmed into 4-inch lengths

¼ lb. green beans, trimmed

2 carrots, peeled and cut into sticks

1 red bell pepper, seeds and ribs removed, and cut into ½-inch slices

1 fennel bulb, trimmed and cut into thin wedges

¼ lb. white mushrooms, wiped clean with a damp paper towel, trimmed, and halved if large

2 to 3 cups olive oil

8 to 10 garlic cloves, peeled and minced

1 (2-oz.) can anchovies, finely chopped, with oil reserved

¼ lb. (1 stick) unsalted butter, cut into pieces

1 TB. freshly squeezed lemon juice

¼ to ½ tsp. red pepper flakes

1. Bring a large pot of salted water to a boil. Blanch broccoli, asparagus, green beans, and carrots for 2 minutes. Drain and plunge vegetables into ice water to stop the cooking action. Drain again.

2. Arrange blanched vegetables on a platter with bell pepper, fennel, and mushrooms. Set aside. (You can do this up to 6 hours in advance and refrigerate it, tightly covered with plastic wrap.)

3. Heat olive oil and reserved anchovy oil in a heavy 2-quart saucepan over medium heat. Add garlic and anchovies, reduce the heat to low, and cook 5 to 7 minutes or until anchovies dissolve. Stir in butter, lemon juice, and red pepper flakes, and cook until butter dissolves. Transfer oil to a ceramic or metal fondue pot or other pot with a heat source. Use a low flame under oil so solids in butter won't burn.

Fondue Facts

Bagna Cauda hails from the Piedmont region of Italy, and the name literally means "hot bath." Garlic and anchovies are constants in the dipping oil, but the other additions can range from fresh herbs to hot pepper flakes.

Variation: Any vegetables from artichoke hearts to zucchini spears can be used in addition to or in place of those listed here.

Vegetarian Falafel Fondue

| Serves: **6** | Prep time: **40 minutes plus 6 hours for soaking** |

1 lb. dried garbanzo beans
1 small onion, peeled and diced
3 garlic cloves, peeled
4 TB. all-purpose flour
2 TB. chopped fresh parsley
1 TB. freshly squeezed lemon juice
1 TB. ground coriander

2 tsp. ground cumin
1 tsp. baking soda
Salt and cayenne to taste
2 cups vegetable oil for frying, plus more as necessary
Suggested sauces: Tahini Sauce, Cucumber Raita, Mexican Tomato Sauce (recipes in Chapter 8)

1. Soak garbanzo beans in cold water to cover for a minimum of 6 hours or preferably overnight. Drain beans and place them in the work bowl of a food processor fitted with a steel blade. Add onion, garlic, flour, parsley, lemon juice, coriander, cumin, baking soda, salt, and cayenne. Process until the mixture forms a smooth paste, scraping the sides of the bowl as necessary.

2. Form paste into 1-inch balls, and refrigerate them 20 minutes, tightly covered with plastic wrap.

3. Heat vegetable oil in a saucepan over medium heat until it reaches 375°F. Transfer oil to a metal fondue pot or other metal pot with a heat source. Cook falafel balls 3 minutes or until browned.

Fondue Facts

Falafel could be considered the french fry of the Middle East, and it's as popular in Israel as it is in Iran and Egypt. It can be made with fava beans, but it's more common to make it with garbanzo beans. What differentiates falafel from other bean patties is that the beans are soaked but not cooked before they're ground into paste.

Chapter 7

Bubbling Broths

In This Chapter

- Traditional Asian broth fondues
- Broth fondues based on European cuisines
- Dishes that are delicious with or without sauce

Broth fondues are a tradition in Asian cooking, but they're relatively unknown in Western countries. We're changing that with the recipes in this chapter. These broths, in which you simmer morsels of meats and seafood, are drawn from many cuisines around the world. While they cook, they'll fill the house with the aroma of herbs and spices as they impart those lively flavors into the food.

These dishes are easy to make and can be assembled hours before you plan on cooking them. They are also very healthful, and while they can be embellished further with dipping sauces, you'll find they're delicious right out of the pot.

Taking Stock

The richer the stock, the better flavor your food will have when it comes out of the fondue pot. If at all possible, use homemade stocks if you have them around. They're as easy to make as boiling water, and they're also inexpensive if you save and freeze scraps from previous meals.

If you don't have homemade stock, use a low-sodium stock and boil it until it's reduced by half before following the stock recipe. This intensifies the stock's flavor, but do be sure the stock is low sodium. Conventional stocks are very high in salt, and if you reduce them to intensify flavor, you'll end up tasting little else but salt.

Infusing the Flavor

The process of adding ingredients to stock and simmering for a short time is called *infusing*. This combines the flavors of the additional ingredients.

It's quick and easy to create an infused stock. There's no need to be dainty about ingredients because they're going to be strained out after the flavor is transferred to the broth. That means the garlic cloves need only be peeled and halved rather than carefully minced, and fresh ginger doesn't even need to be peeled let alone grated. Some ingredients such as onions are briefly sautéed before the broth is added, but most of the time you can start to heat the stock and have the additional ingredients ready to cook before the stock even comes to a boil.

Learning the Level

Because fondue pots and chafing dishes can vary widely, before you start any recipe in this chapter, measure the capacity of the pot you plan to use at the table. You want the level of the broth to half fill the pot, and you also want to reserve some broth to refill the pot as the liquid evaporates during the meal.

You may have to adjust the recipe after you've made this calculation. The stock amounts can be multiplied, but it's doubtful you'll need less than the 4 cups stock you'll get if you make the recipes as written.

Sizing Before Simmering

The boiling temperature of water is only 212°F. That's far lower than the temperature of the oil for the recipes in Chapter 6, and it's also less than specified for most recipes baked in the oven. That means your food must be cut into very thin slices to cook within a reasonable amount of time.

The best way to thinly slice meats and chicken is to place the food in the freezer for 30 minutes to 1 hour, depending on the thickness. A thin flank steak will be brittle in far less time than a thick filet mignon or a whole chicken breast. Your goal is to have the food hard but not frozen. After the food is deep-chilled, it's much easier to cut it into the ¼-inch slices specified in the recipes.

Dip Tips_____

Don't chill shrimp or fish fillets. They cook in such a short amount of time, size isn't as much a problem.

Successful Serving

Chopsticks are a better choice for these broth fondues than a traditional fondue fork. Many of the dishes in this genre have as ingredients delicate, quick-cooking vegetables such as spinach leaves or bean sprouts. These are easier to swirl though the hot broth when held between chopsticks. Chopsticks also make it easier to grasp thin slices of meat.

If you're serving a fondue made with chicken or meat, provide a small plate for each diner for the raw food and then a larger plate on which they can enjoy the food with sauces after the raw food's been cooked. Mixing raw and cooked food could put you at risk for cross-contamination with illness-causing bacteria from the raw food. It's never a wise idea.

Keep an eye on the level of the stock in the fondue pot. Keep additional stock on a low flame in the kitchen so it barely simmers, and refill the pot as necessary to keep the level at half full.

Japanese Beef and Vegetable Fondue with Tamari Broth (*Shabu-Shabu*)

| Serves: **6** | Prep time: **20 minutes** | Cook time: **15 minutes** |

3 cups beef stock

1 cup Japanese soy sauce

4 garlic cloves, peeled and halved

3 TB. thinly sliced fresh ginger

3 scallions, trimmed and sliced

Salt and freshly ground black pepper to taste

1 lb. filet mignon or flank steak, trimmed of all fat and cut into 1/4-inch slices

1/2 lb. firm tofu, cut into 3/4-inch cubes

1/4 lb. spinach leaves, rinsed and stemmed

1/4 lb. fresh shiitake mushrooms, wiped clean with a damp paper towel, rinsed, stemmed, and halved if large

1/4 lb. beans sprouts, rinsed

Suggested sauces: Ponzu Sauce, Thai Sweet and Spicy Dipping Sauce, Sesame Honey Mustard Sauce (recipes in Chapter 8)

1. Combine stock, tamari, garlic, ginger, and scallions in a heavy 2-quart saucepan. Bring to a boil over high heat, stirring occasionally. Reduce heat to medium and simmer stock, uncovered, 15 minutes. Strain stock and season to taste with salt and pepper. (This can be done up to 4 hours ahead. Reheat stock over medium heat until boiling.)

2. While stock is simmering, arrange beef, tofu, spinach, mushrooms, and bean sprouts on a platter. To serve, pour enough strained stock into a metal fondue pot or other metal pot with a heat source to fill it halfway. Reserve any additional stock over low heat for replenishing the pot as needed.

3. Cook beef 1 to 2 minutes or to desired doneness. Cook tofu and vegetables 30 seconds to 1 minute. Serve with desired sauce(s).

Fondue Facts

The name of this dish comes from the swirling sound of cooking the food in the broth. Many Japanese dishes share this name, but this is the most famous one.

Variation: Reduce the soy sauce to 1/2 cup and add 1/2 cup sake to the broth. You can also use slices of chicken or whole raw shrimp in place or in addition to the beef. The chicken should be cooked through and no longer pink.

Moroccan Lamb Fondue with Spiced Tagine Broth

| Serves: **6** | Prep time: **15 minutes** | Cook time: **15 minutes** |

4 cups beef or chicken stock
½ cup chopped fresh parsley
1 TB. ground cumin
1 TB. ground coriander
2 tsp. ground ginger
2 tsp. ground *turmeric*
½ tsp. ground cinnamon
Salt and freshly ground black pepper to taste

1½ lb. lean leg of lamb, trimmed of all fat and cut into ¼-inch slices
¼ lb. white mushrooms, wiped clean with a damp paper towel, trimmed, and halved if large
¼ lb. fresh spinach leaves, rinsed and stemmed
Suggested sauces: Cucumber Raita, Tahini Sauce, Herbed Tomato Sauce (recipes in Chapter 8)

1. Combine stock, parsley, cumin, coriander, ginger, turmeric, and cinnamon in a heavy 2-quart saucepan. Bring to a boil over high heat, stirring occasionally. Reduce heat to medium and simmer stock, uncovered, 15 minutes. Season to taste with salt and pepper. (This can be done up to 4 hours ahead. Reheat stock over medium heat until boiling.)

2. While stock is simmering, arrange lamb, mushrooms, and spinach on a platter. To serve, pour enough stock into a metal fondue pot or other metal pot with a heat source to fill it halfway. Reserve any additional stock over low heat for replenishing the pot as needed.

3. Cook lamb slices 1 to 2 minutes or to desired doneness. Cook mushrooms and spinach 30 seconds to 1 minute. Serve with desired sauce(s).

Variation: Beef or pork can be used in place of the lamb. If using chicken, shrimp, or fish, base the broth on chicken stock rather than beef stock, and be sure the chicken is cooked through and no longer pink.

Dip-Tionary

Turmeric is the root of a tropical plant related to ginger. It has a bitter, pungent flavor and is used to give food a vibrant orange color. It's sometimes called "poor man's saffron" because it adds the same vivid hue—without the cost.

Beef Fondue with Red Wine Broth

| Serves: **6** | Prep time: **15 minutes** | Cook time: **20 minutes** |

1 TB. olive oil

1 small onion, peeled and diced

3 garlic cloves, peeled and halved

3 cups beef stock

1 cup dry red wine

1 sprig fresh thyme or ½ tsp. dried

1 bay leaf

Salt and freshly ground black pepper to taste

1½ lb. filet mignon or flank steak, trimmed of all fat and cut into ¼-inch slices

¼ lb. white mushrooms, wiped clean with a damp paper towel, trimmed, and halved if large

Suggested sauces: Horseradish Sauce, Sun-Dried Tomato Sauce, Easy Aïoli (recipes in Chapter 8)

1. Heat olive oil in a heavy 2-quart saucepan over medium heat. Add onion and garlic and cook, stirring frequently, 3 minutes or until onion is translucent.

2. Add stock, wine, thyme, and bay leaf to the pan. Bring to a boil over high heat, stirring occasionally. Reduce heat to medium, and simmer stock, uncovered, 15 minutes. Strain stock, and season to taste with salt and pepper. (This can be done up to 4 hours ahead. Reheat stock over medium heat until boiling.)

3. While stock is simmering, arrange beef and mushrooms on a platter. To serve, pour enough strained stock into a metal fondue pot or other metal pot with a heat source to fill it halfway. Reserve any additional stock over low heat for replenishing the pot as needed.

Dip Tips

Flank steak is a thin piece of meat and should always be cut across the grain and at an angle to achieve the best slices. You'll see the grain running from top to bottom, so you'll be slicing it across.

4. Cook beef 1 to 2 minutes or to desired doneness. Cook mushrooms 30 seconds to 1 minute. Serve with desired sauce(s).

Variation: Lamb, pork, or veal can be used in place of the beef.

Greek Mixed Meat Fondue with Lemon Oregano Broth

Serves: **6**	Prep time: **15 minutes**	Cook time: **15 minutes**

3 $\frac{1}{4}$ cups beef stock

$\frac{1}{2}$ cup dry red wine

$\frac{1}{4}$ cup freshly squeezed lemon juice

3 TB. tomato paste

$\frac{1}{4}$ cup chopped fresh oregano or 2 TB. dried

3 garlic cloves, peeled and halved

$\frac{1}{4}$ cup chopped fresh parsley

Salt and freshly ground black pepper to taste

$\frac{3}{4}$ lb. boneless leg of lamb, trimmed of all fat and cut into $\frac{1}{4}$-inch slices

$\frac{3}{4}$ lb. filet mignon or flank steak, trimmed of all fat and cut into $\frac{1}{4}$-inch slices

$\frac{1}{4}$ lb. mushrooms, trimmed, wiped clean with a damp paper towel, and halved if large

$\frac{1}{4}$ lb. cherry tomatoes

1 fennel bulb, stalks trimmed, halved, cored, and cut into $\frac{1}{4}$-inch wedges

Suggested sauces: Easy Aïoli, Herbed Tomato Sauce, Cucumber Raita (recipes in Chapter 8)

1. Combine stock, wine, lemon juice, tomato paste, oregano, and garlic in a heavy 2-quart saucepan. Whisk well to dissolve tomato paste. Bring to a boil over high heat, stirring occasionally. Reduce heat to medium, and simmer stock, uncovered, 15 minutes. Strain stock, stir in parsley, and season to taste with salt and pepper. (This can be done up to 4 hours ahead. Reheat stock over medium heat until boiling.)

2. While stock is simmering, arrange lamb, beef, mushrooms, tomatoes, and fennel on a platter. To serve, pour enough strained stock into a metal fondue pot or other metal pot with a heat source to fill it halfway. Reserve any additional stock over low heat for replenishing the pot as needed.

3. Cook lamb, beef, and fennel 1 to 2 minutes or to desired doneness. Cook mushrooms and cherry tomatoes 30 seconds to 1 minute. Serve with desired sauce(s).

Variation: Chicken and shrimp both work well in this recipe. However, if you use these, substitute white wine for the red wine in the broth. Be sure chicken is cooked through and no longer pink.

American Mixed Meat Fondue with Barbecue Broth

Serves: 6 | **Prep time: 15 minutes** | **Cook time: 15 minutes**

2 cups chicken stock

1 cup beef stock

1 cup Southern Barbecue Sauce (recipe in Chapter 8) or bottled barbecue sauce

2 TB. Dijon mustard

1 TB. fresh thyme or 1 tsp. dried

Salt and freshly ground black pepper to taste

$\frac{1}{2}$ lb. filet mignon or flank steak, trimmed of all fat and cut into $\frac{1}{4}$-inch slices

$\frac{1}{2}$ lb. pork tenderloin, trimmed of all fat and silver skin, and cut into $\frac{1}{4}$-inch slices

2 carrots, peeled and sliced on the diagonal into $\frac{1}{4}$-inch slices

2 celery ribs, trimmed and cut on the diagonal into $\frac{1}{4}$-inch slices

$\frac{1}{4}$ lb. green beans, rinsed and stemmed

Suggested sauces: Southern Barbecue Sauce, Louis Sauce, Herbed Tomato Sauce (recipes in Chapter 8)

1. Combine chicken stock, beef stock, barbecue sauce, Dijon mustard, and thyme in a heavy 2-quart saucepan. Bring to a boil over high heat, stirring occasionally. Reduce heat to medium, and simmer stock, uncovered, 15 minutes. Season to taste with salt and pepper. (This can be done up to 4 hours ahead. Reheat stock over medium heat until boiling.)

2. While stock is simmering, arrange beef, pork, carrots, celery, and green beans on a platter. To serve, pour enough strained stock into a metal fondue pot or other metal pot with a heat source to fill it halfway. Reserve any additional stock over low heat for replenishing the pot as needed.

3. Cook all foods for 1 to 2 minutes or to desired doneness. Serve with desired sauce(s).

Fon-Don'ts

The flavor profile of the Southern Barbecue Sauce is sweet and hot. If you use a bottled barbecue sauce, do not use one with a smoky flavor or the broth won't taste right.

Variation: Chicken, shrimp, and fish can be used in place of the beef and pork. If using these foods, use 2 cups chicken stock and 1 cup beef stock rather than the proportion given in the recipe. Be sure chicken is cooked through and no longer pink.

Pork Fondue with Hot and Sour Broth

Serves: 6 | **Prep time: 20 minutes** | **Cook time: 15 minutes**

2 cups chicken stock

1½ cups beef stock

¼ cup rice vinegar

2 TB. Asian sesame oil

2 TB. soy sauce

2 TB. thinly sliced fresh ginger

2 scallions, trimmed and sliced

3 garlic cloves, peeled and halved

1 tsp. red pepper flakes

Salt and freshly ground black pepper to taste

1 lb. pork tenderloin, trimmed of fat and silver skin, and cut into ¼-inch slices

½ lb. firm *tofu*, cut into ¾-inch cubes

¼ lb. fresh shiitake mushrooms, wiped clean with a damp paper towel, stemmed, and halved if large

Suggested sauces: Thai Sweet and Spicy Dipping Sauce, Ponzu Sauce, Spicy Thai Peanut Sauce (recipes in Chapter 8)

1. Combine chicken stock, beef stock, rice vinegar, Asian sesame oil, soy sauce, ginger, scallions, garlic, and red pepper flakes in a heavy 2-quart saucepan. Bring to a boil over high heat, stirring occasionally. Reduce heat to medium, and simmer stock, uncovered, 15 minutes. Strain stock and season to taste with salt and pepper. (This can be done up to 4 hours ahead. Reheat stock over medium heat until boiling.)

2. While stock is simmering, arrange pork, tofu, and mushrooms on a platter. To serve, pour enough strained stock into a metal fondue pot or other metal pot with a heat source to fill it halfway. Reserve any additional stock over low heat for replenishing the pot as needed.

Dip-Tionary

Tofu is also called bean curd on some menus. It's a custard-like food made from curdled soy milk in a process similar to that of cheese-making. The texture depends on how much whey has been pressed out. Be sure to use firm tofu when firm is specified.

3. Cook ingredients for 1 to 2 minutes or to desired doneness. Serve with desired sauce(s).

Variation: Veal, chicken, shrimp, and fish can be substituted for the pork in this recipe. Be sure chicken is cooked through and no longer pink.

Indian Chicken Fondue with Curried Chutney Broth

| Serves: **6** | Prep time: **15 minutes** | Cook time: **15 minutes** |

1 TB. vegetable oil
1 large shallot, peeled and sliced
3 garlic cloves, peeled and halved
4 cups chicken stock
⅓ cup mango chutney
2 TB. thinly sliced fresh ginger
2 TB. curry powder or to taste
1 tsp. ground cumin
Salt and freshly ground black pepper to taste

1½ lb. boneless skinless chicken breast, rinsed and cut into ¼-inch slices
¼ lb. sugar snap peas, rinsed and stemmed
2 carrots, peeled and sliced on the diagonal into ¼-inch slices
Suggested sauces: Cucumber Raita, Tahini Sauce, Thai Sweet and Spicy Dipping Sauce (recipes in Chapter 8)

1. Heat vegetable oil in a heavy 2-quart saucepan over medium heat. Add shallot and garlic, and cook, stirring frequently, 3 minutes or until shallot is translucent.

2. Add stock, chutney, ginger, curry powder, and cumin. Bring to a boil over high heat, stirring occasionally. Reduce heat to medium, and simmer stock, uncovered, 15 minutes. Strain stock and season to taste with salt and pepper. (This can be done up to 4 hours ahead. Reheat stock over medium heat until boiling.)

3. While stock is simmering, arrange chicken, sugar snap peas, and carrots on a platter. To serve, pour enough strained stock into a metal fondue pot or other metal pot with a heat source to fill it halfway. Reserve any additional stock over low heat for replenishing the pot as needed.

> **Fon-Don'ts**
>
> It's possible to substitute a lesser quantity of a dried herb for a fresh one, but never substitute ground ginger for fresh ginger. The flavor profile is far more pungent in any amount.

4. Cook chicken 1 to 2 minutes or until cooked through and no longer pink. Cook sugar snap peas and carrots 30 seconds to 1 minute. Serve with desired sauce(s).

Variation: Shrimp or fish can be substituted for the chicken in this recipe.

Thai Chicken and Shrimp Fondue with Spicy Ginger Broth

| Serves: 6 | Prep time: **15 minutes** | Cook time: **15 minutes** |

4 cups chicken stock

¼ cup fish sauce (*nam pla*)

3 jalapeño chilies, halved

3 TB. thinly sliced fresh ginger

3 garlic cloves, peeled and halved

¼ cup chopped fresh cilantro

Salt and freshly ground black pepper to taste

1 lb. boneless, skinless chicken breast, rinsed and cut into ¼-inch slices

½ lb. extra-large (16 to 20 count) raw shrimp, peeled and deveined

¼ lb. spinach leaves, rinsed and stemmed

6 scallions, trimmed and cut into 1½-inch lengths

8 leaves Napa cabbage, rinsed and cut into 1½-inch lengths

Suggested sauces: Ponzu Sauce, Uncooked Asian Dipping Sauce, Spicy Thai Peanut Sauce (recipes in Chapter 8)

1. Combine stock, fish sauce, chilies, ginger, and garlic in a heavy 2-quart saucepan. Bring to a boil over high heat, stirring occasionally. Reduce heat to medium, and simmer stock, uncovered, 15 minutes. Strain stock, stir in cilantro, and season to taste with salt and pepper. (This can be done up to 4 hours ahead. Reheat stock over medium heat until boiling.)

2. While stock is simmering, arrange chicken, shrimp, spinach, scallions, and cabbage on a platter. To serve, pour enough strained stock into a metal fondue pot or other metal pot with a heat source to fill it halfway. Reserve any additional stock over low heat for replenishing the pot as needed.

3. Cook chicken and shrimp 1 to 2 minutes or until the chicken is cooked through and no longer pink. Cook spinach, scallions, and cabbage 30 seconds to 1 minute. Serve with desired sauce(s).

Variation: Beef, pork, or veal can be used in this recipe. Substitute beef stock for the chicken stock.

Dip Tips

Here's an alternate way to serve Asian broth fondues: cook the meats in the simmering broth and then add the vegetables to the broth and cook them all at once. Then divide the vegetables and broth into soup bowls, and add cooked white rice.

Provençal Seafood Fondue with Saffron Broth

| Serves: **6** | Prep time: **15 minutes** | Cook time: **20 minutes** |

2 TB. olive oil

1 leek, white part only, rinsed and thinly sliced

4 garlic cloves, peeled and halved

½ tsp. saffron threads

2½ cups fish stock or seafood stock

1 (8-oz.) can tomato sauce

½ cup dry white wine

1 TB. herbes de Provence

Salt and freshly ground black pepper to taste

¾ lb. extra-large (16 to 20 count) raw shrimp, peeled and deveined

½ lb. sea scallops, rinsed and halved if large

¼ lb. cherry tomatoes

Suggested sauces: Sun-Dried Tomato Sauce, Easy Aïoli, Herbed Tomato Sauce (recipes in Chapter 8)

1. Heat olive oil in a heavy 2-quart saucepan over medium heat. Add leek and garlic, and cook, stirring frequently, 3 minutes or until leek is translucent. Crush saffron with the back of a teaspoon and set aside.

2. Add stock, tomato sauce, white wine, saffron, and herbes de Provence. Bring to a boil over high heat, stirring occasionally. Reduce heat to medium, and simmer stock, uncovered, 15 minutes. Strain stock, and season to taste with salt and pepper. (This can be done up to 4 hours ahead. Reheat stock over medium heat until boiling.)

3. While stock is simmering, arrange shrimp, scallops, and cherry tomatoes on a platter. To serve, pour enough strained stock into a metal fondue pot or other metal pot with a heat source to fill it halfway. Reserve any additional stock over low heat for replenishing the pot as needed.

4. Cook shrimp and scallops 1 to 2 minutes or to desired doneness. Cook cherry tomatoes 30 seconds to 1 minute. Serve with desired sauce(s).

Variation: Cubes of fish can be substituted for the shrimp and scallops in this recipe.

Fondue Facts

Saffron is the most expensive food in the world, far more dear than truffles or caviar. These yellow-orange stigmas from crocus flowers have to be hand-picked and dried, and there are only three per flower. It takes more than 14,000 stigmas to generate a single ounce of saffron.

Mexican Fish Fondue with Spicy Broth

| Serves: **6** | Prep time: **15 minutes** | Cook time: **20 minutes** |

1 TB. olive oil

1 small onion, peeled and diced

4 garlic cloves, peeled and halved

1 jalapeño chili, seeds and ribs removed, and diced

1 TB. ground cumin

2 tsp. dried oregano

1/2 tsp. red pepper flakes

2 1/2 cups fish stock

1 (8-oz.) can tomato sauce

1/2 cup dry white wine

2 TB. tomato paste

1 bay leaf

1/2 cup chopped fresh cilantro

2 TB. freshly squeezed lime juice

Salt and freshly ground black pepper to taste

1 lb. red snapper or other firm white-fleshed fish fillets, rinsed and cut into 1-inch cubes

1/2 lb. extra-large (16 to 20 count) raw shrimp, peeled and deveined, and rinsed

1/4 lb. cherry tomatoes

1/4 lb. zucchini, trimmed and cut into 1/4-inch slices

Suggested sauces: Creamy Chipotle Sauce, Mexican Tomato Sauce, Uncooked Salsa Sauce (recipes in Chapter 8)

1. Heat olive oil in a heavy 2-quart saucepan over medium heat. Add onion, garlic, and jalapeño pepper. Cook, stirring frequently, 3 minutes or until onion is translucent. Stir in cumin, oregano, and red pepper flakes. Cook, stirring constantly, 1 minute.

2. Stir in fish stock, tomato sauce, white wine, tomato paste, and bay leaf. Stir well to dissolve tomato paste, and bring to a boil over high heat, stirring occasionally. Reduce heat to medium, and simmer stock, uncovered, 15 minutes. Strain stock, stir in cilantro and lime juice, and season to taste with salt and pepper. (This can be done up to 4 hours ahead. Reheat stock over medium heat until boiling.)

3. While stock is simmering, arrange fish, shrimp, cherry tomatoes, and zucchini slices on a platter. To serve, pour enough stock into a metal fondue pot or other metal pot with a heat source to fill it halfway. Reserve any additional stock over low heat for replenishing the pot as needed.

Dip Tips

Fish fall into various categories, the largest being what is dubbed firm-fleshed whitefish. What's most important is the freshness of the fish rather than the species. You could also use halibut, sole, flounder, cod, or whitefish in this recipe.

4. Cook fish and shrimp 1 to 2 minutes or to desired doneness. Cook cherry tomatoes and zucchini 30 seconds to 1 minute. Serve with desired sauce(s).

Variation: Chicken can be substituted for the fish and shrimp in this recipe. Use chicken stock rather than fish stock, and be sure chicken is cooked through and no longer pink.

Chapter 8

Saucy Solutions

In This Chapter

- ◆ Easy mayonnaise-based sauces
- ◆ Creamy sauces for meat, poultry, and fish
- ◆ Low-fat sauces with Asian flavors

Most of the fondue recipes in Chapters 6 and 7 are all enhanced by at least one sauce for dipping after cooking. Here's where you'll find those recipes.

The great part about all these sauces is that they can be prepared in advance, even several days in advance. Another bonus is that many are uncooked compilations of pantry staples that only take minutes to make. That means the pressure's off when planning your fondue fête!

Selecting Your Sauces

All the recipes in Chapters 6 and 7 are annotated with suggestions for which sauces work well for final flavor enhancement. But if you don't like those options, there are a number of alternatives.

Think about the cuisine from which the fondue is drawn. Does it have the refined flavors of Asian food? Is it lusty and Latin? Then refer to the recipes in this chapter and select a sauce or sauces with similar ingredients and flavors. That's all there is to it!

Pantry Pleasures

It can be even easier to select sauces if you look at the contents of your supermarket's refrigerator case and sauce section. These areas have been rapidly growing in recent years, expanding with options as Americans yearn for flavor without fuss.

When shopping, select sauces thick enough to coat the food being dipped after cooking but not so chunky that the flavoring particles won't stick to the food. For example, a ranch dip is fine, but a hearty refrigerated salsa would fall right off.

Here are some other points to keep in mind:

◆ Any dip you'd use with a potato or tortilla chip is perfect fondue fodder, such as ranch dip, blue cheese dip, or our old friend onion dip.

◆ Hummus, the Middle Eastern dip made from garbanzo beans, is now a refrigerated standard. It comes with many flavors, from roasted garlic to lemon.

◆ Thick salad dressings such as creamy Italian or Thousand Island work well.

◆ Barbecue sauces, marinades, and chutneys can be used straight from the bottle.

◆ Dry sauce mixes for hollandaise, béarnaise, and brown sauce variations just need to be prepared according to the instructions on the package and they're ready to go!

Blue Cheese Sauce

| Yield: **2 cups** | Prep time: **10 minutes** |

³/₄ cup mayonnaise
¹/₂ cup sour cream
2 TB. white wine vinegar
¹/₂ lb. blue cheese, crumbled

3 TB. chopped fresh chives
Salt and freshly ground black
pepper to taste

1. Whisk together mayonnaise, sour cream, and vinegar until smooth. Stir in blue cheese and chives, and season to taste with salt and pepper.

2. Refrigerate until ready to use or for up to 4 days.

Variation: To make this sauce lower in fat, substitute nonfat yogurt for both the mayonnaise and sour cream.

Dip Tips

If you don't have any chives, you can always substitute finely chopped scallion tops in a recipe. Don't use the white part of the scallions; they'd be too strong.

Horseradish Sauce

Yield: **2 cups**   Prep time: **10 minutes**

1½ cups crème fraîche
½ cup prepared white horseradish
¼ cup chopped fresh chives
2 TB. freshly squeezed lemon juice

1 tsp. fresh thyme or ¼ tsp. dried
Salt and freshly ground black pepper to taste

1. Combine crème fraîche, horseradish, chives, lemon juice, and thyme in a mixing bowl. Stir well, and season to taste with salt and pepper.

2. Refrigerate until ready to use or for up to 4 days.

Dip Tips

Prepared white horseradish is relatively mild, with the grated root preserved in vinegar. Many gourmet markets today also prepare freshly grated horseradish, which will bring tears to your eyes. Be sure you use the horseradish with lesser intensity.

Dill and Scallion Sauce

| *Yield:* **2 cups** | *Prep time:* **10 minutes** |

1 cup sour cream
³/₄ cup mayonnaise
¹/₄ cup freshly squeezed lemon juice
¹/₃ cup finely chopped scallions

¹/₄ cup chopped fresh dill or 2 TB. dried
2 garlic cloves, peeled and minced
Salt and freshly ground black pepper to taste

1. Whisk together sour cream, mayonnaise, and lemon juice until smooth. Stir in scallions, dill, and garlic. Season to taste with salt and pepper.

2. Refrigerate until ready to use or for up to 4 days.

Dip Tips

When you're using dried rather than fresh herbs in a sauce, try to allow time for the finished recipe to refrigerate for at least 1 hour so the herbs have time to infuse flavor in the food.

Sun-Dried Tomato Sauce

| Yield: **2 cups** | Prep time: **15 minutes** |

½ lb. cream cheese, softened

½ cup mayonnaise

½ cup sour cream

3 garlic cloves, peeled and minced

2 tsp. herbes de Provence

½ cup sun-dried tomatoes packed in oil, drained and diced

4 scallions, trimmed and cut into 1-inch sections

Salt and freshly ground black pepper to taste

1. Combine cream cheese, mayonnaise, sour cream, garlic, and herbes de Provence in a food processor fitted with a steel blade. Purée until smooth. Add sun-dried tomatoes and scallions, and finely chop, using an on-and-off pulsing action. Season to taste with salt and pepper.

2. Refrigerate until ready to use or for up to 4 days.

Dip Tips

Save the oil that's drained off the sun-dried tomatoes. It's wonderful in salad dressings or for making homemade mayonnaise or aïoli.

Easy Aïoli

| Yield: **2 cups** | Prep time: **15 minutes** |

1½ cups mayonnaise

6 garlic cloves, peeled and minced

3 TB. freshly squeezed lemon juice

2 TB. Dijon mustard

Salt and freshly ground black pepper to taste

1. Combine mayonnaise, garlic, lemon juice, and Dijon mustard in a mixing bowl. Whisk well, and season to taste with salt and pepper.

2. Refrigerate until ready to use or for up to 4 days.

Variation: Add 2 tablespoons chili powder or ¼ cup puréed roasted red bell pepper to the basic sauce.

Fondue Facts

While fondue credit is often given to the Swiss, the ancient Greeks might be able to claim the moniker. Homer's *Iliad* (*Song XI*) contains a recipe that's clearly a fondue. The passage discusses a blend of goat cheese with Pramnos wine and flour.

Tartar Sauce

| Yield: **2 cups** | Prep time: **10 minutes** |

1½ cups mayonnaise
¼ cup finely chopped *cornichon*
3 TB. chopped capers
2 TB. white wine vinegar
2 TB. finely chopped shallot

2 TB. chopped fresh parsley
1 TB. chopped fresh tarragon or
1 tsp. dried
Salt and freshly ground black
pepper to taste

1. Combine mayonnaise, cornichon, capers, vinegar, shallot, parsley, and tarragon in a mixing bowl. Whisk well, and season to taste with salt and pepper.

2. Refrigerate until ready to use or for up to 4 days.

Dip-Tionary

Cornichon is the French word for "gherkin," and these sweet-tart pickles made from tiny cucumbers are often seen on a plate with patés or smoked meats. Small gherkin pickles can be substituted, but don't use commercial pickle relish. It just doesn't have the same depth of flavor.

Louis Sauce

| Yield: **2 cups** | Prep time: **10 minutes** |

1½ cups mayonnaise
¼ cup chili sauce
3 scallions, trimmed and finely chopped

3 TB. finely chopped green olives
1 TB. Worcestershire sauce
Salt and freshly ground black pepper to taste

1. Combine mayonnaise, chili sauce, scallions, olives, and Worcestershire sauce in a mixing bowl. Whisk well, and season to taste with salt and pepper.

2. Refrigerate until ready to use or for up to 4 days.

Fondue Facts

Louis sauce is an American concoction from the early twentieth century, but its exact place of birth is a controversy. Some food historians claim it comes from San Francisco, either from the St. Francis Hotel or a now-defunct restaurant named Solari's. Others maintain it was born at Seattle's Olympic Club.

Herbed Tomato Sauce

| Yield: **2 cups** | Prep time: **20 minutes** | Cook time: **45 minutes** |

¼ cup olive oil

1 medium onion, peeled and finely chopped

4 garlic cloves, peeled and minced

1 carrot, peeled and finely chopped

1 celery rib, trimmed and finely chopped

1 (28-oz.) can crushed tomatoes

2 TB. chopped fresh parsley

2 TB. chopped fresh oregano or 2 tsp. dried

1 TB. fresh thyme or 1 tsp. dried

2 bay leaves

Salt and red pepper flakes to taste

1. Heat olive oil in heavy 2-quart saucepan over medium heat. Add onion and garlic, and cook, stirring frequently, 3 minutes or until onion is translucent.

2. Add carrot, celery, tomatoes, parsley, oregano, thyme, and bay leaves. Bring to a boil, reduce heat to low, and simmer sauce uncovered, stirring occasionally, 40 minutes or until lightly thickened. Remove and discard bay leaves, and season to taste with salt and red pepper flakes.

3. Refrigerate for up to 4 days, or freeze it for up to 3 months.

Dip Tips

It's so easy to whip up this sauce that it only makes sense to do a large batch on an occasional basis. If you do, freeze it in different-size containers, ranging from cups (8 fluid ounces) to quarts (32 fluid ounces). That way you'll always have the right amount for any recipe you're making.

Uncooked Salsa Sauce

| Yield: **2 cups** | Prep time: **15 minutes** |

6 ripe plum tomatoes, cored, seeded, and diced

½ small red onion, peeled and diced

½ red or green bell pepper, seeds and ribs removed, and diced

4 garlic cloves, peeled

1 or 2 jalapeño or serrano chilies, seeds and ribs removed

½ cup olive oil

½ cup balsamic vinegar

¼ cup chopped fresh cilantro

Salt and freshly ground black pepper to taste

1. Combine tomatoes, onion, bell pepper, garlic, jalapeño pepper, olive oil, and vinegar in a food processor fitted with a steel blade or in a blender. Pureé until smooth.

2. Scrape mixture into a mixing bowl, stir in cilantro, and season to taste with salt and pepper.

3. Serve at room temperature or chilled. Or refrigerate until ready to use or for up to 2 days.

Dip Tips

Have some leftover Uncooked Salsa Sauce? Easily transform it to a bowl of chilled gazpacho by placing it back in the food processor or blender and adding some peeled and seeded cucumber and tomato juice.

Creamy Chipotle Sauce

Yield: 2 cups | **Prep time: 10 minutes**

1 cup mayonnaise
²/₃ cup sour cream
3 TB. freshly squeezed lime juice
3 scallions, trimmed and chopped
3 garlic cloves, peeled and minced

3 *chipotle chilies* in adobo sauce, finely chopped
1 tsp. adobo sauce
Salt to taste

1. Combine mayonnaise, sour cream, lime juice, scallions, garlic, chipotle chilies, and adobo sauce in a mixing bowl. Whisk well, and season to taste with salt.

2. Refrigerate until ready to use or for up to 4 days.

Dip Tips

A can of chipotle chilies in adobo sauce goes a long way. Chances are you use less than a half-dozen chilies in a given recipe. To save the remainder of the can, place a few chilies with a teaspoon of sauce in ice-cube trays. When they're frozen, transfer them to a heavy resealable plastic bag. Be sure to wash the ice-cube tray well.

Mexican Tomato Sauce

| Yield: **2 cups** | Prep time: **15 minutes** | Cook time: **20 minutes** |

3 TB. olive oil

1 small onion, peeled and finely chopped

3 garlic cloves, peeled and minced

2 to 3 TB. chili powder

1 TB. ground cumin

$^3/_4$ cup chicken stock or vegetable stock

1 (15-oz.) can tomato sauce

1 (4-oz.) can chopped mild green chilies, drained

$^1/_4$ cup chopped fresh cilantro

Salt and freshly ground black pepper to taste

1. Heat olive oil in a heavy 2-quart saucepan over medium heat. Add onion and garlic, and cook, stirring frequently, 3 minutes or until onion is translucent. Reduce heat to low, stir in chili powder and cumin, and cook, stirring constantly, 1 minute.

2. Stir in stock, tomato sauce, and green chilies. Whisk well, bring to a boil, and simmer, uncovered, 15 minutes, stirring occasionally, or until sauce is reduced by $^1/_4$.

3. Stir in cilantro, and season to taste with salt and pepper. Serve hot or at room temperature. (Sauce can be made up to 4 days in advance and refrigerated, tightly covered. Reheat to at least room temperature before serving.)

Dip Tips

Chili powder is a commercial blend of many dried herbs and spices, and frequently salt as well. When using it, be sure to taste a dish before seasoning with additional salt. You may find that none is needed, depending on the brand of chili powder you use.

Indonesian Barbecue Sauce

Yield: **2 cups**	Prep time: **10 minutes**	Cook time: **20 minutes**

1½ cups pineapple juice
¾ cup distilled white vinegar
⅓ cup soy sauce
¼ cup finely chopped fresh ginger

¾ cup ketchup
⅓ cup firmly packed dark brown sugar
¼ cup chopped fresh cilantro
⅓ cup freshly squeezed lime juice

1. Combine pineapple juice, vinegar, soy sauce, and ginger in a saucepan. Bring to a boil over medium-high heat, and boil 15 minutes or until liquid is reduced by ½, stirring occasionally.

2. Add ketchup and brown sugar to the pan, reduce heat to low, and simmer sauce 5 minutes. Remove the pan from heat, and stir in cilantro and lime juice.

3. Ladle sauce into containers, and refrigerate until ready to use or for up to 2 weeks.

Dip Tips

Sugar and ingredients that contain sugar are added at the end of the cooking process to keep the sauce from scorching as it boils. That's also why barbecue sauce should only be basted on food for the last few moments it's grilled.

Sesame Honey Mustard Sauce

| Yield: **2 cups** | Prep time: **10 minutes** |

1 cup Dijon mustard
$^2/_3$ cup honey

$^1/_2$ cup Asian sesame oil
$^1/_2$ cup chopped fresh cilantro

1. Combine Dijon mustard, honey, Asian sesame oil, and cilantro in a mixing bowl. Whisk until smooth.

2. Refrigerate until ready to use or for up to 4 days.

Fondue Facts

Dijon mustard does indeed hail from Dijon, France, and one of the leading manufacturers at its home base is Poupon, makers of Grey Poupon. The seasonings may vary, but Dijon mustard must contain both white wine and unfermented white grape juice to be Dijon.

Uncooked Asian Dipping Sauce

Yield: 2 cups   *Prep time:* **10 minutes**

³/₄ cup unsweetened applesauce
¹/₂ cup *hoisin sauce*
¹/₄ cup firmly packed dark brown sugar
6 TB. ketchup

2 TB. honey
2 TB. rice vinegar
1 TB. soy sauce
1 TB. Chinese chili sauce (or hot red pepper sauce)

1. Combine applesauce, hoisin sauce, brown sugar, ketchup, honey, rice vinegar, soy sauce, and Chinese chili sauce in a mixing bowl. Whisk until smooth.

2. Refrigerate until ready to use, or for up to 1 week.

Dip Tips

To save time when making a recipe with many liquid ingredients, measure them into the same large cup, calculating what the level should be after each addition.

Spicy Thai Peanut Sauce

Yield: **2 cups**	Prep time: **10 minutes**

1 cup chunky peanut butter

$^1/_2$ cup hot water

$^1/_2$ cup firmly packed dark brown sugar

$^1/_3$ cup freshly squeezed lime juice

$^1/_4$ cup soy sauce

2 TB. Asian sesame oil

2 TB. Asian chili sauce

6 garlic cloves, peeled and minced

3 scallions, trimmed and chopped

$^1/_4$ cup chopped fresh cilantro

1. Combine peanut butter, water, brown sugar, lime juice, soy sauce, Asian sesame oil, and Asian chili sauce in a mixing bowl. Whisk until well combined.

2. Stir in garlic, scallions, and cilantro.

3. Refrigerate until ready to use or for up to 4 days.

Fondue Facts

Peanuts are used in cuisines around the world, but peanut butter is a home-grown American invention. It was developed in 1890 and first promoted as a health food at the 1904 World's Fair in St. Louis.

Cucumber Raita

| Yield: **2 cups** | Prep time: **10 minutes** |

$\frac{1}{2}$ medium cucumber, peeled, seeded, and finely chopped

2 ripe plum tomatoes, cored, seeded, and finely chopped

2 scallions, trimmed and finely chopped

2 garlic cloves, peeled and minced

1 cup plain whole-milk yogurt

2 TB. chopped fresh dill or 2 tsp. dried

2 TB. freshly squeezed lemon juice

Salt and freshly ground black pepper to taste

1. Combine cucumber, tomatoes, scallions, garlic, yogurt, dill, and lemon juice in a mixing bowl. Stir well, and season to taste with salt and pepper.

2. Refrigerate until ready to use or for up to 2 days.

Dip-Tionary

Raita is the generic name given to yogurt-based Indian sauces designed to cool down spicy dishes. They can contain a variety of raw or cooked vegetables and fruits and also herbs and spices. Similar sauces are used in many Mediterranean cuisines.

Tahini Sauce

| Yield: **2 cups** | Prep time: **10 minutes** |

²/₃ cup tahini paste
²/₃ cup water
¹/₂ cup freshly squeezed lemon
juice

3 garlic cloves, peeled
Salt and cayenne to taste

1. Combine tahini paste, water, lemon juice, garlic, salt, and cayenne in a blender. Blend until smooth, scraping the inside of the jar as necessary.

2. Refrigerate until ready to use or for up to 4 days.

Dip Tips

Tahini paste is made from ground sesame seeds, and it has a tendency to separate in the container. Be sure you stir it well before measuring. You may have to transfer it to a mixing bowl to stir if the container is very full.

Thai Sweet and Spicy Dipping Sauce

Yield: 2 cups   **Prep time: 10 minutes**

1 cup rice vinegar

²/₃ cup fish sauce (*nam pla*)

¹/₃ cup firmly packed dark brown sugar

6 garlic cloves, peeled and minced

1¹/₂ tsp. crushed red pepper flakes or to taste

1. Combine vinegar, fish sauce, dark brown sugar, garlic, and red pepper flakes in a jar with a tight-fitting lid. Shake until sugar is dissolved.

2. Serve at room temperature or chilled. Or refrigerate until ready to use or for up to 4 days.

Dip Tips

Brown sugar is granulated sugar mixed with molasses, and the darker the color, the more pronounced the molasses flavor. If a recipe calls for dark brown sugar, and you only have light brown sugar, add 2 tablespoons molasses per ¹/₂ cup sugar to replicate the taste.

Ponzu Sauce

| Yield: **2 cups** | Prep time: **10 minutes** |

$\frac{1}{2}$ cup soy sauce
$\frac{1}{2}$ cup *mirin*
$\frac{1}{2}$ cup freshly squeezed lemon juice

$\frac{1}{4}$ cup Asian sesame oil
3 TB. grated fresh ginger
1 TB. grated lemon zest

1. Combine soy sauce, mirin, lemon juice, Asian sesame oil, ginger, and lemon zest in a jar with a tight-fitting lid. Shake well.

2. Refrigerate for up to 4 days.

Dip-Tionary

Mirin is a sweet Japanese wine made from glutinous rice, and it's part of many traditional dishes. If you can't find it, you can substitute sweet sherry in a pinch, adding 1 tablespoon granulated sugar to each $\frac{1}{4}$ cup liquid.

Dippity Do!

Dips are the foundation of American entertaining—and with good reason. They're easy to eat. Dip, dunk, or scoop is all you have to do and you're chewing. There's no fork, no plate, and no fuss.

It's recipes for delicious hot dips that you'll find in Part 4. Many of these dips also contain cheese, but a dip is thicker than a fondue. It's fun to serve different types of dips at a party, and the dips in this part run the gamut.

Chapter 9 is devoted to vegetarian dips, many of which are also vegan. In Chapter 10, you'll find dips including a variety of meats, and seafood is the star of the dips in Chapter 11.

9

Vibrant and Vegetarian

In This Chapter

◆ Dips drawn from ethnic cuisines
◆ Dips combining vegetables and cheeses
◆ Dips starring low-fat ingredients

I've covered fondues up to this point, but here's where we get into dips! What's the difference, you ask? Lots! Dips are casual party food, easy for guests to eat. In general, dips are thicker than a fondue, even if they contain cheese. This is true of hot as well as cold dips. And dips use food as the fork; there's no cutlery involved.

An assortment of dips today should always include vegetarian options, and that's what you'll find in this chapter. All the dips here are vegetarian, but many of them contain dairy products so they're not vegan.

Strong and Sturdy Dippers

Due to their thick consistency, the foods used to scoop dips have to be sturdy. It's embarrassing for a guest to break off a delicate food in the bowl of dip, and it's equally distressing for a dipper to collapse on the way from the bowl to the waiting mouth and the dip ends up on a dress or tie.

All the recipes in this chapter are annotated with suggestions as to what foods to serve with the dips, but here are some general guidelines:

♦ Foods should be wide enough to hold the dip but short enough so they can be eaten in one bite. A rectangle of red bell pepper is preferable to a long thin strip, and a small oval cracker is a better choice than a long breadstick.

♦ Carbohydrate foods should be sturdy rather than brittle and retain their texture when wet. A potato chip or delicate puff pastry cheese straw can become soggy and collapse in a bowl of hot dip. Crackers or tortilla chips are better choices.

♦ Raw, blanched, or cooked vegetables should be crunchy, not supple. Sugar snap peas are nice with a thin cold dip; a wedge of jicama or a carrot stick are better with hot dips.

Successful Serving

The easiest way to serve dips and keep them hot is in a fondue pot or any of the options discussed in Chapter 1. Small slow cookers work especially well for dips—dessert fondues, too! (More on dessert fondues in Part 5.)

If you're using a ceramic pot, you can heat it in a 375°F oven for 1 hour. That will create enough heat to keep a dip hot for at least an hour without any additional heat source. For a longer party, use the stand that comes with the ceramic pot but be sure it's on a solid surface so the pot won't tip off when people dip into it.

Few people own more than one ceramic fondue pot, but you can still serve more than one hot dip at a party by heating low, ovenproof glass or porcelain bowls in the same way you would heat a ceramic fondue pot. If it can go into the oven, it can become a serving dish.

For a more novel look, hollow out a loaf of bread, leaving at least a 2-inch case. Toast the bread in a 350°F oven until it's very dry and crusty, at least 1 hour. Immediately fill it with hot dip. The dip will remain hot and the bread won't get soggy.

Fon-Don'ts

Watch where you put the hot pot! Always place a trivet or at least a folded dish towel underneath a hot pot to protect the table or counter surface beneath it. It's also a good idea to place dip bowls on a large napkin. This prevents the dip from falling on the furniture or table linens. The napkin can be changed from time to time to keep the setting neat.

Artichoke and Parmesan Dip

Serves: 8 to 10 | *Prep time:* **15 minutes** | *Cook time:* **5 minutes**

1 cup freshly grated Parmesan cheese

²/₃ cup mayonnaise

¹/₂ cup sour cream

2 TB. freshly squeezed lemon juice

2 TB. chopped fresh parsley

1 TB. fresh thyme or 1 tsp. dried

1 garlic clove, peeled and minced

3 scallions, white part only, trimmed and cut into ¹/₂-inch pieces

2 (10 oz.) pkg. frozen artichoke hearts, thawed and drained

Salt and freshly ground black pepper to taste

1. Combine Parmesan cheese, mayonnaise, sour cream, lemon juice, parsley, thyme, and garlic in a heavy 2-quart saucepan. Stir well.

2. Place scallions and artichoke hearts in the bowl of a food processor fitted with a steel blade. Chop finely using an on-and-off pulsing action. Scrape the mixture into the saucepan, stir well, and season to taste with salt and pepper. (You can do this up to 2 days in advance and refrigerate, tightly covered.)

3. Place the saucepan over medium heat and cook, stirring occasionally, 5 minutes or until the mixture is bubbly and hot.

4. Transfer dip to a fondue pot or other heated serving dish, and serve with crostini, pita crisps, bagel chips, or crudités.

Fondue Facts

Artichokes do not pair well with wine because they contain cynarin, a bioactive substance that reacts with food eaten immediately afterward causing it to take on a sweet taste. The cheese in this recipe mitigates that effect.

Spinach Dip with Feta and Dill

| Serves: **8 to 10** | Prep time: **15 minutes** | Cook time: **6 minutes** |

2 (10-oz.) pkg. frozen chopped spinach, thawed

2 TB. unsalted butter

1 medium onion, peeled and chopped

1 garlic clove, peeled and minced

$\frac{1}{2}$ lb. (2 cups) crumbled *feta cheese*

1 (3-oz.) pkg. cream cheese, softened

$\frac{1}{4}$ cup chopped fresh dill or 3 TB. dried

2 TB. chopped fresh oregano or 2 tsp. dried

3 TB. freshly squeezed lemon juice

Salt and freshly ground black pepper to taste

1. Place spinach in a colander or strainer, and press with the back of a spoon to extract as much liquid as possible.

2. Heat butter in a large skillet over medium heat. Add onion and garlic, and cook, stirring frequently, 3 minutes or until onion is translucent.

3. Stir spinach, feta cheese, cream cheese, dill, oregano, and lemon juice into the skillet. Reduce heat to low, and cook, stirring frequently, until mixture comes to a boil. Simmer 3 minutes, stirring occasionally. Season to taste with salt and pepper.

4. Transfer dip to a fondue pot or other heated serving dish, and serve with crostini, pita crisps, cooked tortellini, cooked gnocchi, or crudités.

Dip-Tionary

Feta cheese is a classic Greek cheese traditionally made from sheep or goat milk, although today it's often made with cow's milk. White, crumbly, and rindless, feta is usually pressed into square cakes. It has a rich, tangy flavor and can range in texture from soft to semidry.

Cauliflower and Cheddar Dip

| Serves: **8 to 10** | Prep time: **10 minutes** | Cook time: **10 minutes** |

2 (1-lb.) bags frozen cauliflower
½ lb.
(2 cups) shredded sharp or mild cheddar cheese
½ cup half-and-half

1 tsp. dry mustard
1 tsp. sweet paprika
Salt and freshly ground black pepper to taste

1. Cook cauliflower in a heavy 2-quart saucepan according to package instructions, adding 2 minutes to the cooking time or cooking until cauliflower is very soft. Drain well in a colander.

2. Return cauliflower to the saucepan over low heat. Add cheese, half-and-half, mustard, and paprika. Mash cauliflower with a potato masher until well blended and cheese is melted. Season to taste with salt and pepper. (You can do this up to 2 days in advance and refrigerate, tightly covered. Reheat it in a microwave oven until hot.)

Fondue Facts

Humorist Mark Twain gave cauliflower a boost when he wrote, "cauliflower is nothing but cabbage with a college education." The name comes from two Latin words: *caulis*, means "stalk," and *floris*, or "flower."

3. Transfer dip to a fondue pot or other heated serving dish, and serve with crudités, crostini, crispy potato wedges, or rice crackers.

Variation: Chopped broccoli can be substituted for the cauliflower, and either Swiss cheese or Monterey Jack cheese can be substituted for the cheddar.

Caramelized Onion and Gruyère Dip

Serves: **8 to 10** | *Prep time:* **15 minutes** | *Cook time:* **45 minutes**

3 TB. unsalted butter

3 TB. olive oil

4 large (2 lb.) Vidalia or other sweet onions, peeled and diced

2 garlic cloves, peeled and minced

Salt and freshly ground black pepper to taste

2 tsp. granulated sugar

1 TB. fresh thyme or 1 tsp. dried

1 cup dry white wine

1½ lb. Gruyère cheese, grated

3 TB. cold water

1 TB. cornstarch

1. Heat butter and olive oil in a large skillet over medium heat. Add onion and garlic, and toss to coat. Cover the pan, reduce heat to low, and *sweat* onions for 10 minutes. Uncover the pan, and sprinkle onions with salt, pepper, sugar, and thyme. Raise the heat to medium-high, and cook, stirring occasionally, 20 to 30 minutes or until onions are well browned. (You can do this up to 2 days in advance and refrigerate, tightly covered.)

2. Add wine to the skillet and bring to a boil. Add cheese to wine by ½ cup measures, stirring constantly with a whisk in a figure-eight pattern. Add additional cheese only after the previous addition is melted.

3. Combine water and cornstarch in a small bowl, and stir to dissolve cornstarch. Add to the skillet, and bring to a simmer, stirring constantly. Cook over low heat 1 to 2 minutes or until dip has thickened. Season to taste with salt and pepper.

4. Transfer dip to a fondue pot or other heated serving dish, and serve with crispy potato wedges, pita crisps, crostini, bagel chips, or crudités.

Dip-Tionary

Sweating is a technique by which vegetables are cooked, covered, in a small amount of fat over low heat so the ingredients soften without browning and cook in their own juices.

Mango, Green Chili, and Brie Dip

| Serves: **8 to 10** | Prep time: **15 minutes** | Cook time: **15 minutes** |

2 TB. unsalted butter

1 medium onion, peeled and diced

2 garlic cloves, peeled and minced

1 lb. Brie cheese, softened

¼ cup heavy cream

2 fresh mangoes, peeled and chopped

2 (4-oz.) cans chopped mild green chilies, drained

Salt and freshly ground black pepper to taste

1. Melt butter in a heavy 2-quart saucepan over medium-low heat. Add onion and garlic, and cook, stirring frequently, 5 to 8 minutes or until onion is soft.

2. Scrape top rind off Brie, and scoop out interior cheese using a spoon. Discard bottom and side rinds.

Fon-Don'ts

Be careful when buying green chilies. The mild green chilies are right next to the fiery jalapeño peppers. Look for the word *mild* on the label, or just be sure the label doesn't say *jalapeño*.

3. Add Brie and cream to the saucepan, and stir until cheese is melted and bubbly. Stir in mangoes and green chilies, and season to taste with salt and pepper.

4. Transfer dip to a fondue pot or other heated serving dish, and serve with baked tortilla chips, fresh jicama, crostini, or crudités.

Provençal Mixed Vegetable Dip (Ratatouille)

| Serves: **8 to 10** | Prep time: **20 minutes** | Cook time: **1 hour** |

2 (1-lb.) eggplants

3 TB. olive oil

2 large onions, peeled and chopped

4 garlic cloves, peeled and minced

3 medium red bell peppers, seeds and ribs removed, and finely chopped

2 medium zucchini, trimmed and cut into ¼-inch dice

2 medium yellow squash, trimmed and cut into ¼-inch dice

3 TB. fresh thyme or 1 TB. dried

Salt and freshly ground black pepper to taste

1 (14-oz.) can diced tomatoes, drained

3 TB. chopped fresh parsley

1. Preheat the oven to 450°F. Rinse eggplants under cold water, and prick them with a sharp meat fork or the tip of a paring knife. Bake 20 minutes, turn, and bake an additional 20 minutes or until flesh is very soft when poked with a meat fork.

2. When eggplants are cool enough to handle, slice them in half and scrape out flesh. Add any juices from the baking pan. Purée in a food processor fitted with a steel blade. (You can do this up to 2 days in advance and refrigerate, tightly covered.)

3. Heat olive oil in a large skillet over medium-high heat. Add onions and garlic, and cook, stirring frequently, 3 minutes or until onion is translucent. Add bell peppers, zucchini, squash, thyme, salt, and pepper. Cook, stirring occasionally, 8 to 10 minutes or until vegetables are tender.

4. Add tomatoes and cook, stirring occasionally, 3 minutes. Stir in eggplant and parsley, and season to taste with more salt and pepper.

5. Transfer dip to a fondue pot or other heated serving dish, and serve with pita chips, short breadsticks, crostini, or crudités.

Dip Tips

Male eggplants are sweeter than female because they have far fewer bitter seeds. To tell the difference, look at the base of the eggplant. The male has a rounded bottom with a smooth stem area while the female eggplant is more elliptical, with a deeply indented stem area.

Spicy Chinese Eggplant Dip with Water Chestnuts and Scallions

| *Serves:* **8 to 10** | *Prep time:* **15 minutes** | *Cook time:* **1 hour** |

2 (1-lb.) eggplants

6 garlic cloves, peeled and minced

2 TB. grated fresh ginger

6 scallions, trimmed and thinly sliced

$\frac{1}{2}$ to 1 tsp. dried red pepper flakes

$\frac{1}{3}$ cup soy sauce

$\frac{1}{4}$ cup firmly packed dark brown sugar

2 TB. unseasoned Japanese rice vinegar

2 TB. hot water

2 TB. vegetable oil

2 TB. Asian sesame oil

1 (8-oz.) can water chestnuts, drained, rinsed, and chopped

1. Preheat the oven to 450°F. Rinse eggplants under cold water, and prick them with a sharp meat fork or the tip of a paring knife. Bake 20 minutes, turn, and bake an additional 20 minutes or until flesh is very soft when poked with a meat fork.

2. When eggplants are cool enough to handle, slice them in half and scrape out flesh. Add any juices from the baking pan. Purée in a food processor fitted with a steel blade. (You can do this up to 2 days in advance and refrigerate, tightly covered.)

3. Combine garlic, ginger, scallions, and red pepper flakes in a small dish. Combine soy sauce, brown sugar, vinegar, and water in another small bowl, stirring to dissolve sugar.

4. Heat a wok or large heavy skillet over high heat. Add vegetable oil and Asian sesame oil, swirl to glaze the pan, and reduce heat to moderately high. Add scallion mixture, and stir-fry 15 seconds. Add liquid mixture, and stir until simmering. Add eggplant and water chestnuts, and bring to a simmer.

Dip Tips

Asian stir-frying is like a game of *Beat the Clock;* it all moves very fast from the get-go. That's why it's so important to have all ingredients measured and combined with others going into the dish at the same time.

5. Transfer dip to a fondue pot or other heated serving dish, and serve with wonton crisps, rice crackers, crostini, or crudités.

Garlicky Garbanzo Bean Dip with Roasted Red Peppers

| Serves: **8 to 10** | Prep time: **10 minutes** | Cooking time: **10 minutes** |

2 roasted red bell peppers, peeled, seeded, and diced

2 (15-oz.) cans garbanzo beans, drained and rinsed

$\frac{1}{3}$ cup olive oil

$\frac{1}{4}$ cup freshly squeezed lemon juice

5 garlic cloves, peeled and minced

$\frac{1}{2}$ cup chopped fresh parsley

1 TB. fresh thyme or 1 tsp. dried

Salt and freshly ground black pepper to taste

1. Place roasted peppers in the work bowl of a food processor fitted with a steel blade. Chop finely using an on-and-off pulsing action. Scrape peppers into a heavy 2-quart saucepan.

2. Combine beans, olive oil, lemon juice, and garlic in the food processor. Purée until smooth. Scrape mixture into the saucepan, and add parsley and thyme. Season to taste with salt and pepper.

3. Place the saucepan over medium heat. Cook, stirring frequently, until the mixture comes to a boil and bubbles.

4. Transfer dip to a fondue pot or other heated serving dish, and serve with pita crisps, short breadsticks, crostini, or crudités.

Dip Tips

This dip isn't fat-free, but it's certainly high in heart-healthy, mono-unsaturated fats. Try it chilled as an alternative to mayonnaise on various sandwiches. It's especially good with grilled chicken.

Variation: White beans or pinto beans can be used in place of the garbanzo beans.

Mexican Black Bean Dip

| *Serves:* **8 to 10** | *Prep time:* **15 minutes** | *Cooking time:* **10 minutes** |

$\frac{1}{3}$ cup olive oil

1 onion, peeled and chopped

4 garlic cloves, peeled and minced

2 (15-oz.) cans black beans, drained and rinsed

$\frac{1}{2}$ cup crème fraîche

$\frac{1}{4}$ cup freshly squeezed lime juice

1 tsp. ground coriander

1 tsp. ground cumin

1 TB. chopped fresh oregano or 1 tsp. dried

1 tsp. red pepper sauce or to taste

$\frac{1}{2}$ cup chopped pimiento

$\frac{1}{4}$ cup chopped fresh cilantro

Salt and freshly ground black pepper to taste

1. Heat olive oil in a large skillet over medium heat. Add onion and garlic, and cook, stirring constantly, 3 minutes or until onion is translucent. Set aside.

2. Combine beans, crème fraîche, lime juice, coriander, cumin, oregano, and red pepper sauce in a food processor fitted with a steel blade. *Purée* until smooth, and scrape the mixture into the skillet. Stir in pimiento and cilantro, and bring to a simmer over medium heat, stirring frequently. Season to taste with salt and pepper.

3. Transfer dip to a fondue pot or other heated serving dish, and serve with baked tortilla wedges, slices of fresh jicama, crostini, or crudités.

Dip-Tionary

Purée means to turn foods to a thick, creamy texture resembling thick baby food. The most efficient way to do this is with a food processor. Unless there's a lot of liquid, a blender isn't really up to the job.

Asian Butternut Squash Dip

| Serves: **8 to 10** | Prep time: **10 minutes** | Cook time: **15 minutes** |

3 (10-oz.) pkg. frozen butternut or winter squash, thawed

¹/₃ cup freshly squeezed orange juice

3 TB. unsalted butter

¹/₂ cup hoisin sauce

1 tsp. grated orange zest

¹/₂ tsp. Chinese five-spice powder

Salt and freshly ground black pepper to taste

1. Cook squash according to package directions in a large saucepan. Mash squash with a potato masher until smooth.

2. Add orange juice, butter, hoisin sauce, orange zest, and Chinese five-spice powder. Stir well, and cook over low heat, stirring frequently, until butter is melted and dip is bubbly. Season to taste with salt and pepper.

3. Transfer dip to a fondue pot or other heated serving dish, and serve with wonton crisps, slices of fresh jicama, crostini, or crudités.

Dip Tips

There's virtually no difference between acorn or butternut squash in flavor, color, or texture, so you can use them interchangeably in recipes. Some brands of frozen squash just refer to the product as "winter squash" for that reason.

Chapter 10

The Meat of the Matter

In This Chapter

- ◆ Dips containing meat and poultry
- ◆ Latin America–flavored dips
- ◆ Saucy dips with cheeses and cream

In some ways, the dip recipes in this chapter can be considered a meal in themselves. They're hearty while not being heavy, and if some vegetables are used for dipping, you've got all necessary nutrients in one dish.

These dips truly span the globe. Some feature Asian flavors, others draw from Latin American cuisines, and some are great-tasting homegrown variations on American classics.

Loving Leftovers

Hot dips are a great way to use up leftovers when you might not have enough to create a whole meal for the family. If you want to use leftover meats, chop them to the consistency of ground meat. This can easily be done in a food processor fitted with the steel blade using quick on and off pulses.

Another bonus: using cooked meats make the preparation times for these dips much faster, too!

Easy Subbing

If you have extra chicken but a recipe calls for turkey, don't turn the page! Chicken and turkey can be used interchangeably in any of these recipes.

You can use leftover meats in place of the uncooked ones specified, too, especially grilled hamburgers. They lend a wonderful smoky note to any dip.

Pork and Tomatillo Dip

| Serves: **8 to 10** | Prep time: **10 minutes** | Cook time: **20 minutes** |

1 TB. olive oil
1 lb. lean ground pork
1 onion, peeled and diced
2 garlic cloves, peeled and minced
2 jalapeño chilies, seeds and ribs removed, and finely chopped
1 lb. *tomatillos*, husks removed, rinsed, cored, and finely chopped

³/₄ cup chicken stock
1 TB. granulated sugar
1 TB. tequila
1 TB. cornstarch
¹/₄ cup chopped fresh cilantro
Salt and freshly ground black pepper to taste

1. Heat olive oil in a large skillet over medium-high heat. Add pork and cook, breaking up lumps with a fork, 3 to 5 minutes or until pork is no longer pink. Remove pork from the pan with a slotted spoon, and set aside. Discard all but 2 tablespoons grease from the pan.

2. Return the pan to the heat, and add onion, garlic, and jalapeños. Cook, stirring frequently, for 3 minutes or until onion is translucent. Return pork to the pan, and add tomatillos, chicken stock, and sugar. Bring to a boil, reduce the heat to medium, and cook for 10 minutes or until tomatillos are soft.

3. Combine tequila and cornstarch in a small bowl, and stir to dissolve cornstarch. Add to dip, and bring to a simmer, stirring constantly. Cook over low heat for 1 to 2 minutes or until dip has thickened. (This can be done up to 4 hours ahead. Reheat over medium heat until boiling.) Stir in cilantro, and season to taste with salt and pepper.

4. Transfer dip to a fondue pot or other heated serving dish, and serve with tortilla chips, crostini, pita crisps, or crudités.

Dip-Tionary

Tomatillos, sometimes called Mexican green tomatoes, have a flavor that's a cross between tart apple, lemon, and herbs. They are small and covered with a parchmentlike covering that should be removed before cooking.

Chorizo and Pinto Bean Dip

Serves: 8 to 10 | **Prep time: 10 minutes** | **Cook time: 15 minutes**

1 TB. olive oil
½ lb. bulk *chorizo*
1 onion, peeled and diced
3 garlic cloves, peeled and minced
2 jalapen~o chilies, seeds and ribs removed, and finely chopped
1 TB. ground cumin

1 (14-oz.) can petite diced tomatoes, undrained
1 (15-oz.) can pinto beans, drained and rinsed
¼ lb. (1 cup) Monterey Jack cheese, coarsely grated
Salt and freshly ground black pepper to taste

1. Heat olive oil in a large skillet over medium-high heat. Add chorizo and cook, breaking up lumps with a fork, for 3 to 5 minutes or until sausage is no longer pink. Remove chorizo from the pan with a slotted spoon and set aside. Discard all but 2 tablespoons grease from the pan.

2. Return the pan to the heat, and add onion, garlic, and jalapeños. Cook, stirring frequently, for 3 minutes or until onion is translucent. Stir in cumin, and cook for 30 seconds. Add tomatoes and pinto beans, and return sausage to the pan. Cook over medium heat for 5 minutes. Stir in cheese, and cook until cheese is melted.

Dip-Tionary

Chorizo is a garlicky sausage containing chili powder and other spices that's used in many Mexican and Spanish dishes. The pork is coarsely ground, which makes it an excellent choice for dips.

3. Use a potato masher to mash mixture until about ½ beans are mashed. Season to taste with salt and pepper. (This can be done up to 4 hours ahead. Reheat over medium heat until boiling.)

4. Transfer dip to a fondue pot or other heated serving dish, and serve dip with tortilla chips, plantain chips, crostini, pita crisps, or crudités.

Mexican Beef and Chili Dip (Chili con Queso)

| Serves: **8 to 10** | Prep time: **10 minutes** | Cook time: **15 minutes** |

2 TB. olive oil

1 onion, peeled and diced

3 garlic cloves, peeled and minced

1 lb. lean ground beef

1 (15-oz.) can petite cut diced tomatoes, drained

1 (4-oz.) can chopped mild green chilies, drained

$\frac{1}{2}$ cup heavy cream

$\frac{1}{2}$ lb. (2 cups) Monterey Jack cheese, coarsely grated

$\frac{1}{2}$ lb. (2 cups) cheddar cheese, coarsely grated

1 TB. cold water

1 TB. cornstarch

Salt and freshly ground black pepper to taste

1. Heat olive oil in a large heavy skillet over medium-high heat. Add onion, garlic, and ground beef. Cook, breaking up lumps with a fork, for 3 to 5 minutes or until beef is brown and no pink remains. Add tomatoes and green chilies, and cook for an additional 3 minutes. Remove the contents of the skillet with a slotted spoon, and discard grease from the skillet.

2. Return the contents to the skillet, and add cream and Monterey Jack and cheddar cheeses. Cook over medium heat, stirring frequently, for 3 minutes or until cheese is melted and bubbly.

3. Combine water and cornstarch in a small bowl, and stir to dissolve cornstarch. Add to dip, and bring to a simmer, stirring constantly. Cook over low heat for 1 to 2 minutes or until dip has thickened. Season to taste with salt and pepper. (This can be done up to 4 hours ahead. Reheat over medium heat until boiling.)

4. Transfer dip to a fondue pot or other heated serving dish, and serve the dip with tortilla chips, plantain chips, crostini, pita crisps, or crudités.

Dip Tips

Petite cut tomatoes are a relative newcomer to the market, and they're great for dips. Regular diced tomatoes should really be cut into smaller pieces or someone's dip into the bowl could yield nothing but a tomato. The petite cut ones are preferable and save time.

Asian Pork and Vegetable Dip

| Serves: **8 to 10** | Prep time: **20 minutes** | Cook time: **15 minutes** |

2 TB. Asian sesame oil

4 scallions, trimmed and chopped

4 garlic cloves, peeled and minced

3 TB. finely chopped fresh ginger

1 lb. lean ground pork

$\frac{1}{2}$ red bell pepper, seeds and ribs removed, and finely chopped

2 celery ribs, trimmed, rinsed, and finely chopped

1 (8-oz.) can water chestnuts, drained, rinsed, and finely chopped

$\frac{1}{2}$ cup chicken stock

$\frac{1}{4}$ cup soy sauce

3 TB. black bean sauce with garlic

2 TB. rice vinegar

2 TB. sherry

1 TB. cold water

1 TB. cornstarch

$\frac{1}{4}$ cup chopped fresh cilantro

Salt and freshly ground black pepper to taste

1. Heat Asian sesame oil in a large heavy skillet over medium heat. Add scallions, garlic, and ginger, and cook, stirring constantly, for 30 seconds. Add pork, breaking up lumps with a fork, and cook for 3 to 5 minutes or until pork is no longer pink.

2. Add red bell pepper, celery, and water chestnuts to the skillet, and cook for 3 minutes, stirring constantly. Add chicken stock, soy sauce, black bean sauce, rice vinegar, and sherry. Bring to a boil, and simmer for 5 minutes. (This can be done up to 4 hours ahead. Reheat over medium heat until boiling.)

3. Combine water and cornstarch in a small bowl, and stir to dissolve cornstarch. Add to fondue, and bring to a simmer, stirring constantly. Cook over low heat for 1 to 2 minutes or until fondue has thickened. Stir in cilantro, and season to taste with salt and pepper.

Fon-Don'ts

Not all rice vinegar is created equal. The ones already seasoned are intended as condiments and should not be used for cooking.

4. Transfer dip to a fondue pot or other heated serving dish, and serve with wonton crisps, crostini, pita crisps, or crudités.

Variation: Ground turkey can be substituted for the pork in this recipe.

Cheeseburger Dip

| Serves: **8 to 10** | Prep time: **15 minutes** | Cook time: **15 minutes** |

2 TB. olive oil

1 onion, peeled and diced

3 garlic cloves, peeled and minced

1 lb. lean ground beef

1 (15-oz.) can petite cut diced tomatoes, drained

4 TB. unsalted butter

$\frac{1}{4}$ cup all-purpose flour

$\frac{3}{4}$ cup half-and-half

$\frac{1}{2}$ lb. (2 cups) mild or sharp cheddar cheese, coarsely grated

Salt and freshly ground black pepper to taste

1. Heat olive oil in a large heavy skillet over medium-high heat. Add onion, garlic, and ground beef. Cook, breaking up lumps with a fork, for 3 to 5 minutes or until beef is brown and no pink remains. Add tomatoes and cook for an additional 3 minutes. Remove the contents of the skillet with a slotted spoon, and discard grease from the skillet.

2. Melt butter in the skillet over medium heat. Reduce the heat to low, add flour, and cook for 2 minutes, stirring constantly.

3. Raise the heat to medium, and whisk in half-and-half. Bring to a boil, whisking until smooth. Stir meat mixture into sauce, and simmer for 5 minutes, stirring frequently. Add cheese, and cook until cheese is melted. Season to taste with salt and pepper. (This can be done up to 4 hours ahead. Reheat over medium heat until boiling.)

3. Transfer dip to a fondue pot or other heated serving dish, and serve with crostini, pita crisps, bagel chips, or crudités.

Fondue Facts

References to hamburgers date back to the nineteenth century, when residents of Hamburg, New York, claim they were invented in 1885 for the Erie County Fair. By 1904, when they were served at the Louisiana Purchase Exposition in St. Louis, Missouri, hamburgers were truly national. References to cheeseburgers don't start until just prior to World War II.

Hoppin' John Dip

| Serves: **8 to 10** | Prep time: **15 minutes** | Cook time: **10 minutes** |

2 TB. olive oil

½ onion, peeled and diced

¼ red bell pepper, seeds and ribs removed, and chopped

1 celery rib, trimmed, rinsed, and chopped

3 garlic cloves, peeled and minced

½ lb. cooked ham, trimmed of all visible fat and chopped

1 TB. fresh thyme or 1 tsp. dried

1 (15-oz.) can black-eyed peas, drained and rinsed

1 (3-oz.) pkg. cream cheese, softened

Salt and freshly ground black pepper to taste

1. Heat olive oil in a large heavy skillet over medium-high heat. Add onion, bell pepper, celery, and garlic. Cook, stirring frequently, for 3 minutes or until onion is translucent.

2. Add ham, thyme, and black-eyed peas to the skillet, reduce the heat to medium, and cook for 2 minutes or until ham is hot. Stir in cream cheese, and season to taste with salt and pepper. (This can be done up to 4 hours ahead. Reheat over medium heat until boiling.)

3. Transfer dip to a fondue pot or other heated serving dish, and serve with tortilla chips, crostini, pita crisps, or crudités.

Fondue Facts

Hoppin' John is first mentioned in culinary history in 1838, and no self-respecting Southerner would end New Year's Day without having a bowl of black-eyed peas. It means good luck for the whole year. The name comes from the practice of children hopping around the table once before eating the dish.

Sausage Pizza Dip

| Serves: **8 to 10** | Prep time: **10 minutes** | Cook time: **15 minutes** |

1 TB. olive oil
1 lb. mild or hot Italian bulk sausage
1 cup spaghetti sauce
1 tsp. dried oregano

1 tsp. dried basil
$\frac{1}{2}$ tsp. dried thyme
1 lb. (4 cups) whole milk mozzarella cheese, coarsely grated
Salt and freshly ground black pepper to taste

1. Heat olive oil in a large skillet over medium-high heat. Add sausage and cook, breaking up lumps with a fork, for 3 to 5 minutes or until sausage is no longer pink. Remove sausage from the skillet with a slotted spoon, and discard grease from the pan.

2. Return sausage to the pan, and add spaghetti sauce, oregano, basil, and thyme. Bring to a boil, reduce the heat to low, and simmer sauce for 10 minutes or until slightly thickened. Stir in cheese, and cook until cheese is melted. Season to taste with salt and pepper. (This can be done up to 4 hours ahead. Reheat over medium heat until boiling.)

3. Transfer dip to a fondue pot or other heated serving dish, and serve with crostini, pita crisps, bagel chips, or crudités.

Variation: You can personalize this recipe in many ways according to your favorite pizza toppings. Ground beef or diced pepperoni can be used in place of the sausage, or you can make this a vegetarian dip by adding sautéed onion, green pepper, or mushrooms.

Fon-Don'ts

If you can't find bulk sausage for recipes, add a few minutes to the prep time for removing the sausage meat from its casings.

All you have to do is push on one end like a tube of toothpaste, but it's important to do it because the casing turns into nasty rubber bands when cooked.

Southern Creamed Sausage Dip

Serves: 8 to 10 | **Prep time: 10 minutes** | **Cook time: 15 minutes**

1 lb. bulk pork sausage
2 garlic cloves, peeled and minced
¼ cup all-purpose flour

1 TB. dried sage
1 cup half-and-half
Salt and freshly ground black pepper to taste

1. Heat a large heavy skillet over medium-high heat. Add sausage, breaking up lumps with a fork, and cook for 5 to 7 minutes or until no longer pink. Remove sausage from the pan with a slotted spoon, and discard all but 3 tablespoons sausage grease.

2. Return the pan to medium heat, and add garlic. Cook, stirring constantly, for 30 seconds. Reduce the heat to low, add flour, and cook for 2 minutes, stirring constantly. Add sage and cook for 30 seconds.

3. Raise the heat to medium, and whisk in half-and-half. Bring to a boil, whisking until smooth. Stir sausage into sauce, and simmer for 5 minutes, stirring frequently. Season to taste with salt and pepper. (This can be done up to 4 hours ahead. Reheat over medium heat until boiling.)

4. Transfer dip to a fondue pot or other heated serving dish, and serve with flour tortilla chips, crostini, pita crisps, bagel chips, or crudités.

Dip Tips

If you use a dairy product with less butterfat than the half-and-half specified in this recipe, increase the flour by 2 tablespoons. One of the qualities of cream is that it serves as a thickener, which skim milk will not.

Chicken Tetrazzini Dip

| Serves: **8 to 10** | Prep time: **15 minutes** | Cook time: **20 minutes** |

7 TB. unsalted butter

2 TB. olive oil

$\frac{1}{2}$ lb. white mushrooms, wiped clean with a damp paper towel, trimmed, and diced

3 scallions, trimmed with all but 2 inches of green tops discarded, and sliced

2 garlic cloves, peeled and minced

$\frac{1}{4}$ cup all-purpose flour

1 cup half-and-half

$\frac{1}{4}$ cup sherry

1 TB. fresh thyme or 1 tsp. dried

$\frac{1}{2}$ lb. cooked chicken, chopped

$\frac{1}{3}$ cup freshly grated Parmesan cheese

Salt and freshly ground black pepper to taste

1. Heat 3 tablespoons butter and olive oil in a large skillet over medium-high heat. Add mushrooms, scallions, and garlic. Cook, stirring frequently, for 3 to 5 minutes or until mushrooms are soft. Set aside.

2. Melt remaining 4 tablespoons butter in a heavy 2-quart saucepan over medium heat. Reduce the heat to low, add flour, and cook for 2 minutes, stirring constantly. Raise the heat to medium, and whisk in half-and-half, sherry, and thyme. Bring to a boil, whisking until smooth. Simmer sauce for 3 minutes, stirring frequently.

Fondue Facts

Chicken Tetrazzini is named for famed opera singer Luisa Tetrazzini, who was extremely popular in the early twentieth century. In her autobiography, she couldn't recall who actually created the dish in her honor but noted that she seemed to be served it in every city she toured.

3. Stir in mushrooms, chicken, and Parmesan cheese, and season to taste with salt and pepper. (This can be done up to 4 hours ahead. Reheat over medium heat until boiling.)

4. Transfer dip to a fondue pot or other heated serving dish, and serve with crostini, pita crisps, bagel chips, or crudités.

Turkey and Asparagus Dip

| *Serves:* **8 to 10** | *Prep time:* **15 minutes** | *Cook time:* **10 minutes** |

1 (10-oz.) pkg. frozen asparagus
4 TB. unsalted butter
¼ cup all-purpose flour
½ cup chicken stock
½ cup heavy cream
1 TB. chopped fresh *tarragon* or 1 tsp. dried

½ lb. cooked turkey, chopped
¼ lb. (1 cup) Swiss cheese, coarsely grated
Salt and freshly ground black pepper to taste

1. Cook asparagus according to package directions. Drain well and chop.

2. Melt butter in a heavy 2-quart saucepan over medium heat. Reduce the heat to low, add flour, and cook for 2 minutes, stirring constantly. Raise the heat to medium, and whisk in chicken stock and cream. Bring to a boil, whisking until smooth. Stir in tarragon, and simmer sauce for 3 minutes, stirring frequently.

3. Stir in asparagus, turkey, and Swiss cheese, and season to taste with salt and pepper. (This can be done up to 4 hours ahead. Reheat over medium heat until boiling.)

4. Transfer dip to a fondue pot or other heated serving dish, and serve with crostini, pita crisps, bagel chips, or crudités.

Dip-Tionary

Tarragon is one of the most popular herbs in classic French cooking because its rich aroma and pungent aniselike flavor blends so well with poultry and vegetable dishes, especially asparagus.

Chapter 11

Sensational Seafood

In This Chapter

- ◆ Dips from the sea
- ◆ Ethnic-inspired dips
- ◆ Easy dips made with precooked seafood

The popularity of fish and seafood continues to grow, so it's only natural that these aquatic protein sources serve as a draw to the dip bowl. Those are the recipes you'll find in this chapter.

A great advantage of seafood dips is that in almost all these recipes, the seafood ingredient is already cooked. That makes these dips as easy to make as they are delicious to eat!

Species Substitutions

These seafood-y recipes are open to a lot of substitution. You can swap crab for shrimp, shrimp for crab, or either for clams in any recipe as you see fit. All these species have a mild, almost sweet flavor.

If you're substituting one for another, use the same weight and prepare the seafood as dictated in a similar recipe. For example, crab needs only to be picked over, while even tiny shrimp should be diced into smaller pieces. Follow the instructions for the type of fish you're using, and you're all set.

Successful Serving

These recipes have been formulated to be ready to eat in the least amount of time possible. But you can also create a different visual and textural presentation by baking the dips.

Preheat the oven to 350°F and grease a 2-quart oven-proof casserole or soufflé dish. Follow the procedure for combining ingredients; however, you can do it in a mixing bowl.

You'll bake the dip for about 30 minutes or until it's bubbly, but before you slide it into the oven, have some fun with it. Sprinkle some sort of crunchy mixture on the top of the casserole. Breadcrumbs with a few tablespoons grated Parmesan cheese added in are a good bet for dips with European ancestry. For dips with Asian inspiration, use *panko* crumbs. Crushed tortilla chips are the best choice for Hispanic dips.

Dip-Tionary

Panko are Japanese breadcrumbs that are lighter, longer, and less dense than typical breadcrumbs. This texture creates a deliciously crunchy crust on baked or fried foods.

Crab Rangoon Dip

| Serves: **8 to 10** | Prep time: **15 minutes** | Cook time: **5 minutes** |

1 (8-oz.) pkg. cream cheese, softened

$\frac{1}{2}$ cup coconut milk

3 scallions, trimmed with all but 2 inches green tops discarded, and chopped

2 garlic cloves, peeled and minced

2 TB. soy sauce

2 TB. grated fresh ginger

1 TB. Worcestershire sauce

$\frac{1}{2}$ lb. crabmeat, picked over well

2 TB. chopped fresh cilantro

Salt and freshly ground black pepper to taste

1. Combine cream cheese, coconut milk, scallions, garlic, soy sauce, ginger, and Worcestershire sauce in a heavy 2-quart saucepan. Cook over medium-low heat, stirring frequently, for 5 minutes or until mixture is hot and bubbly.

2. Stir in crabmeat and cilantro. Season to taste with salt and pepper.

3. Transfer dip to a fondue pot or other heated serving dish, and serve with wonton Crab Rangoon Dipcrisps, crostini, pita crisps, bagel chips, or crudités.

Fondue Facts

Crab Rangoon was popularized in the 1950s at the Trader Vic's chain of Polynesian restaurants that sprang up across the country. Capitalizing on the popularity of movies such as *South Pacific* as well as thousands of soldiers returning from serving in the region, the restaurants featured exotic rum drinks and appetizers dubbed Pu-Pu.

Crab and Salsa Dip

Serves: 8 to 10 | **Prep time: 15 minutes** | **Cook time: 5 minutes**

1 pt. refrigerated salsa, either hot or mild depending on personal preference
1 (8-oz.) pkg. cream cheese, softened

³/₄ cup mayonnaise
¹/₄ cup chopped fresh cilantro
2 tsp. ground cumin
¹/₂ lb. crabmeat, picked over well
Salt and cayenne to taste

1. Place salsa in a colander, and shake it well to remove excess liquid. Combine salsa, cream cheese, mayonnaise, cilantro, and cumin in a heavy 2-quart saucepan. Cook over medium-low heat, stirring frequently, for 5 minutes or until mixture is hot and bubbly.

Fon-Don'ts

The salsa you should use for this dip is the fresh, refrigerated product found either in the produce aisle or with the cheeses. The taste and texture of jarred salsa just don't work with this dish.

2. Stir in crabmeat, and season to taste with salt and cayenne.

3. Transfer dip to a fondue pot or other heated serving dish, and serve with tortilla chips, crostini, pita crisps, bagel chips, or crudités.

Thai Crab and Coconut Dip

| Serves: **8 to 10** | Prep time: **15 minutes** | Cook time: **5 minutes** |

1 (8-oz.) pkg. cream cheese, softened

½ cup coconut milk

3 scallions, trimmed with all but 2 inches green tops discarded, and chopped

2 garlic cloves, peeled and minced

¼ cup chopped fresh cilantro

1 jalapeño chili, seeds and ribs removed, and finely chopped

3 TB. fish sauce (*nam pla*)

½ lb. crabmeat, picked over well

Salt and freshly ground black pepper to taste

1. Combine cream cheese, coconut milk, scallions, garlic, cilantro, jalapeño, and fish sauce in a heavy 2-quart saucepan. Cook over medium-low heat, stirring frequently, for 5 minutes or until mixture is hot and bubbly.

2. Stir in crabmeat, and season to taste with salt and pepper.

3. Transfer dip to a fondue pot or other heated serving dish, and serve with plantain chips, wonton crisps, crostini, pita crisps, or crudités.

Dip Tips

Even with the most sophisticated of machinery, it's difficult to rid crabmeat of all shell fragments. The easiest way to pick it over is on a dark-colored plate. Spread it around gently with your fingers so you won't break up the prized morsels, and you'll see the shell fragments.

Herbed Shrimp, Artichoke, and Brie Dip

| Serves: **8 to 10** | Prep time: **15 minutes** | Cook time: **15 minutes** |

1 (10-oz.) pkg. frozen artichoke hearts

3 TB. unsalted butter

1 leek, white part only, chopped and well rinsed

2 garlic cloves, peeled and minced

$\frac{1}{3}$ cup dry white wine

$\frac{1}{3}$ cup heavy cream

1 lb. (4 cups) Brie cheese, at room temperature

2 TB. chopped fresh parsley

1 TB. chopped fresh tarragon or 1 tsp. dried

$\frac{1}{2}$ lb. cooked salad shrimp (at least 40 count), coarsely diced

Salt and freshly ground black pepper to taste

1. Cook artichokes according to package directions. Drain them well, and coarsely chop them.

2. Heat butter in a heavy 2-quart saucepan over medium heat. Add leek and garlic, and cook, stirring frequently, for 5 minutes or until leek is soft. Add wine and cream to the pan, raise the heat to medium-high, and cook for 5 minutes or until liquid is reduced by $\frac{1}{3}$.

3. Scrape the top rind off brie, and scoop out interior cheese using a spoon. Discard bottom and side rinds. Add Brie to the pan slowly, stirring so that each addition is melted before adding the next.

4. Stir in parsley, tarragon, and shrimp. Season to taste with salt and pepper.

5. Transfer dip to a fondue pot or other heated serving dish, and serve with crostini, pita crisps, bagel chips, or crudités.

Fondue Facts

Catherine de' Medici is credited for bringing artichokes from her native Italy to France (along with table cutlery) when she married King Henry II in the fifteenth century. They were an instant hit. The Italian and French explorers then introduced them to California, the state that now produces 100% of the U.S. commercial artichokes.

Cajun Shrimp Dip

Serves: **8 to 10** | *Prep time:* **15 minutes** | *Cook time:* **10 minutes**

2 TB. unsalted butter
$\frac{1}{2}$ onion, peeled and finely chopped
1 celery stalk, rinsed, trimmed, and finely chopped
$\frac{1}{4}$ green bell pepper, seeds and ribs removed, and finely chopped

1 (8-oz.) pkg. cream cheese, softened
$\frac{3}{4}$ cup mayonnaise
1 TB. *Cajun seasoning*
$\frac{1}{2}$ lb. cooked salad shrimp (at least 45 count), coarsely diced

1. Heat butter in a heavy 2-quart saucepan over medium heat. Add onion, celery, and green pepper. Cook, stirring frequently, for 3 to 5 minutes or until onion is translucent.

2. Add cream cheese, mayonnaise, and Cajun seasoning. Cook over medium-low heat, stirring frequently, for 5 minutes or until mixture is hot and bubbly. Stir in shrimp, and season to taste with additional Cajun seasoning.

3. Transfer dip to a fondue pot or other heated serving dish, and serve with crostini, pita crisps, bagel chips, or crudités.

Dip-Tionary

Cajun seasoning is a relative newcomer to the spice aisle. Generally, it contains garlic, onions, cayenne, black pepper, chili, mustard, paprika, thyme, and oregano, but each blend is slightly different.

Curried Shrimp Dip

Serves: 8 to 10 | **Prep time: 15 minutes** | **Cook time: 10 minutes**

½ cup slivered almonds

1 (8-oz.) pkg. cream cheese, softened

½ cup mayonnaise

½ cup mango chutney, finely chopped

2 TB. *curry powder*

½ lb. cooked salad shrimp (at least 45 count), coarsely diced

½ cup dried apricots, chopped

Salt and freshly ground black pepper to taste

1. Toast almonds in a 350°F oven for 5 to 7 minutes or until lightly browned. Chop and set aside.

2. Combine cream cheese, mayonnaise, chutney, and curry powder in a heavy 2-quart saucepan. Cook over medium-low heat, stirring frequently, for 5 minutes or until mixture is hot and bubbly.

Dip-Tionary

Curry powder is actually a blend of up to 20 spices, herbs, and seeds. Among them are always cardamom, chilies, cinnamon, coriander, black pepper, and turmeric. The hotter "Madras" powders also contain cayenne, and other mixes also include saffron and fennel seed.

3. Stir in shrimp, almonds, and dried apricots. Season to taste with salt and pepper.

4. Transfer dip to a fondue pot or other heated serving dish, and serve with toasted Indian naan bread, crostini, pita crisps, or crudités.

Mexican Clam Dip

Serves: 8 to 10 | **Prep time: 15 minutes** | **Cook time: 10 minutes**

2 TB. unsalted butter

2 shallots, peeled and chopped

3 garlic cloves, peeled and minced

1 (8-oz.) pkg. cream cheese, softened

$\frac{1}{4}$ lb. (1 cup) jalapeño Jack cheese, grated

$\frac{1}{2}$ cup green chili salsa (*salsa verde*)

$\frac{1}{4}$ cup chopped fresh cilantro

3 (6.5-oz.) cans chopped clams, drained well

Salt and freshly ground black pepper to taste

1. Heat butter in a heavy 2-quart saucepan over medium heat. Add shallots and garlic, and cook, stirring frequently, for 3 minutes or until shallots are translucent.

2. Stir in cream cheese, jalapeño Jack, salsa, cilantro, and clams. Cook over medium-low heat, stirring frequently, for 5 minutes or until mixture is hot and bubbly. Season to taste with salt and pepper.

3. Transfer dip to a fondue pot or other heated serving dish, and serve with tortilla chips, crostini, pita crisps, bagel chips, or crudités.

Dip Tips

Jalapeño Jack is a great convenience because the hot peppers are right there in the cheese, but if all you have around is Monterey Jack, just add 1 finely chopped fresh jalapeño pepper to the pan when you're sautéing the shallots and garlic.

Clam Rockefeller Dip

| *Serves:* **8 to 10** | *Prep time:* **15 minutes** | *Cook time:* **10 minutes** |

2 TB. olive oil

1 small onion, peeled and chopped

3 garlic cloves, peeled and minced

2 (6.5-oz.) cans minced clams, undrained ½ cup heavy cream

1 TB. Pernod (or other licorice-flavored liqueur)

½ (10-oz.) pkg. frozen chopped spinach, thawed and drained

1 (8-oz.) pkg. cream cheese, softened

3 TB. freshly grated Parmesan cheese

Salt and freshly ground black pepper to taste

1. Heat oil in a heavy 2-quart saucepan over medium heat. Add onion and garlic, and cook, stirring frequently, for 3 minutes or until onion is translucent.

2. Add clams with their liquid, cream, and Pernod to the pan, and bring to a boil. Add spinach and cook for 2 minutes. Add cream cheese and Parmesan cheese, and cook, stirring constantly, until cheese is melted and mixture is smooth. Season to taste with salt and pepper.

Fondue Facts

This dip is a variation on Oysters Rockefeller, a dish born in 1899 at New Orleans' Antoine's restaurant. At the time getting snails from Europe was a problem, so the chef, Jules Alciatore, concocted the dish to take the place of escargot.

3. Transfer dip to a fondue pot or other heated serving dish, and serve with crostini, pita crisps, bagel chips, or crudités.

Dilled Salmon Dip with Smoked Salmon

| Serves: **8 to 10** | Prep time: **15 minutes** | Cook time: **15 minutes** |

1 (³/₄-lb.) salmon fillet, rinsed and patted dry with paper towels

1 TB. Old Bay seasoning

12 oz. cream cheese, softened

3 TB. freshly squeezed lemon juice

2 TB. white horseradish

¼ lb. smoked salmon, finely chopped

4 scallions, trimmed and finely chopped

2 TB. chopped fresh dill or 2 tsp. dried

Freshly ground black pepper to taste

1. Rub salmon with Old Bay seasoning and place it on a microwave-safe dish. Cover the dish with plastic wrap, and microwave salmon on high (100 percent) for 3 minutes or until cooked through. Cut a slit in the plastic wrap for the steam to escape and then discard the plastic wrap. Discard salmon skin, if necessary, and break salmon into 1-inch chunks. Reserve any juices.

2. Combine salmon, any accumulated juices, cream cheese, lemon juice, and horseradish in a food processor fitted with a steel blade or in a blender. Process until smooth, and scrape mixture into a heavy 2-quart saucepan.

3. Stir smoked salmon, scallions, and dill into mixture. Cook over medium-low heat, stirring frequently, for 5 minutes, or until mixture is hot and bubbly. Season to taste with pepper.

4. Transfer dip to a fondue pot or other heated serving dish, and serve with crostini, pita crisps, bagel chips, or crudités.

Fon-Don'ts

I know it's tempting to use canned salmon rather than cooking a fresh fillet, and I even tried it a few times. But the flavor and texture of the dip just wasn't the same. Take the extra few minutes, and don't substitute in this recipe.

Variation: The salmon can also be cooked in a 450°F oven, covered with foil, for 15 minutes.

Herbed Sole Dip

| Serves: **8 to 10** | Prep time: **15 minutes** | Cook time: **15 minutes** |

$^1\!/_2$ lb. fillet of sole or other firm-fleshed whitefish

Salt and freshly ground black pepper to taste

2 TB. unsalted butter

2 shallots, peeled and minced

2 garlic cloves, peeled and minced

1 (5.2-oz.) pkg. Boursin cheese with herbs and garlic

1 (3-oz.) pkg. cream cheese, softened

$^1\!/_4$ cup *crème fraîche*

$^1\!/_4$ cup mayonnaise

3 TB. chopped fresh parsley

3 TB. chopped fresh chives or 1 TB. dried

1 TB. chopped fresh tarragon or 1 tsp. dried

1. Season sole with salt and pepper, and place it on a microwave-safe dish. Cover the dish with plastic wrap, and microwave sole on high (100 percent) for 2 minutes or until cooked through. Cut a slit in the plastic wrap for the steam to escape and then discard the plastic wrap. Chop sole finely either by hand or in a food processor fitted with a steel blade using on-and-off pulsing.

2. While fish is cooking, heat butter in a heavy 2-quart saucepan over medium heat. Add shallots and garlic, and cook, stirring frequently, for 3 minutes or until shallots are translucent.

3. Add sole, Boursin, cream cheese, crème fraîche, mayonnaise, parsley, chives, and tarragon to the saucepan. Cook over medium-low heat, stirring frequently, for 5 minutes or until mixture is hot and bubbly. Season to taste with salt and pepper.

Dip-Tionary

Crème fraîche is a thickened cream with a tangy flavor similar to that of sour cream. It's used extensively in cooking because it does not curdle as sour cream does when heated to boiling.

4. Transfer dip to a fondue pot or other heated serving dish, and serve with crostini, pita crisps, bagel chips, or crudités.

Part **5**

Decadent Desserts

Dessert fondues are a fast and fabulous way to end a meal. They're fun to eat and incredibly easy to make, as the recipes in Part 5 demonstrate.

Chapter 12 is where you'll find luscious chocolate confections. Various types of chocolate are melted with myriad ingredients that add their flavors and textures. Within minutes you have an elegant ending.

For those times you want to make dessert memorable with other flavors, look no further than Chapters 13 and 14. In the former, other classic dessert flavors like caramel and butterscotch star, and fruits to suit every fancy are featured in the last chapter.

Chapter 12

Chocolate Cravings

In This Chapter

- ◆ Basic chocolate fondue
- ◆ Sensuous fruit-and-nut fondues
- ◆ Candy bar fondues? Yep!

Many people believe that the *only* responsibility of a dessert is that it be chocolate. And there's no easier, or more elegant, chocolate dessert than a chocolate fondue. It's ready in a matter of minutes, and with a little care, making it is foolproof. Those are the kinds of recipes you'll find in this chapter.

Chocolate fondues can be personalized in myriad ways. Just changing the liqueur from one to another adds flavor nuances, and additional ingredients also increase the textural interest. Some of the fondues in this chapter replicate popular combinations found in chocolate candy bars; others are luscious liquid versions of rich chocolate truffles.

Chocolate 101

The key to success for all chocolate fondues is to use a high-quality chocolate as the base. Many domestic as well as imported chocolates meet this definition. Look for a high percentage of cocoa butter, and you can't go wrong.

Now on to the sweet stuff. Here's a quick guide to chocolate:

Unsweetened   Also referred to as baking, bitter, chocolate, this is the purest of all cooking chocolate, containing no added ingredients such as milk or sugar. It's usually packaged in a bar of 8 (1-ounce) blocks.

Bittersweet   This chocolate, usually between 25 and 50 percent cocoa, is slightly sweetened with sugar—and mainly used for baking. It should be used when intense chocolate flavor is desired.

Semisweet   This chocolate is sweetened with sugar, but unlike bittersweet, it also can have added flavorings such as vanilla. Semisweet chocolate is usually American; bittersweet is most often imported.

Sweet cooking   This chocolate contains 15 percent chocolate liquor, and it almost always has a higher sugar content than semisweet chocolate. It is usually found in 4-ounce bars.

Milk   This is a mild-flavored chocolate used primarily for candy bars but rarely (except for milk chocolate chips) in cooking. To qualify as milk chocolate, it can have as little as 10 percent chocolate liquor but must contain 12 percent milk solids.

Fondue Facts

Chef Konrad Egli created chocolate fondue. The dish first appeared on his menu at New York's Chalet Swiss, a restaurant that popularized all fondue on this side of the Atlantic Ocean, in 1964.

White   Actually ivory in color, white chocolate is technically not chocolate at all; it is made from sweetened cocoa butter, milk solids, sugar, and vanilla flavoring and contains no chocolate liquor.

Always wrap chocolate tightly after it's opened because it can absorb aromas and flavors from other foods. Store chocolate in a cool, dry place, but do not refrigerate or freeze it. If chocolate is stored at a high temperature, the fat will rise to the surface and become a whitish powder called a bloom. This will disappear, however, as soon as the chocolate is melted, so there's no reason not to use it in a fondue.

Like red wine, chocolate ages and becomes more deeply flavored after 6 months and can be kept for years if stored properly. However, because of the milk solids in both milk chocolate and white chocolate, these shouldn't be stored for longer than 9 months.

Handle with Care

When you're making a chocolate fondue, the chocolate needs a bit of special handling.

First, chop the chocolate into fine pieces to make melting easier. You can do this in a food processor fitted with a steel blade. Begin by breaking it with a heavy knife rather than with your hands. Body heat is sufficiently high enough to soften the chocolate so it won't chop evenly. If you don't have a food processor, place small chunks of chocolate in a heavy resealable plastic bag, cover the bag with a dish towel, and chop it by hitting it with the bottom of a heavy saucepan.

Chocolate needs careful melting because it scorches easily. When making chocolate fondue, there's frequently some type of liquid along with the chocolate, but you still need to take care. You can simply place the chocolate into a saucepan, but if you want some alternative ways of making the fondue ...

- Microwave chopped chocolate in a microwave-safe bowl on high (100 percent) for 20 seconds. Stir, and repeat as necessary.

- Preheat the oven to 250°F. Place chopped chocolate in the oven and then turn off the heat immediately. Stir after 3 minutes and return to the warm oven if necessary.

- Combine the chocolate and cream in a heatproof bowl, and place it on the warming surface of an electric coffee maker.

Note: Although all the recipes in this chapter give the "Stir over very low heat" instruction for melting the chocolate, you can employ any of these methods if you prefer. Try a new method each time you make chocolate fondue and decide which you like best!

Successful Serving

You took special care when you melted your fondue chocolate, and that same care should be used when serving the finished fondue. Chocolate fondue should be placed over very low heat to keep it hot but not allow it to scorch.

If you're serving the fondue from a chafing dish or metal fondue pot, it's best to use a votive candle rather than an alcohol burner or other hot fuel source. The best choice for serving chocolate fondue is the small dip-size slow cooker discussed in Chapter 1.

Classic Chocolate Fondue

| *Serves:* **6** | *Prep time:* **10 minutes** | *Cook time:* **5 minutes** |

½ cup heavy cream

10 oz. bittersweet chocolate, chopped

2 to 3 TB. liquor or liqueur (your favorite: rum, bourbon, tequila, Cognac, brandy, triple sec, Grand Marnier, Chambord, kirsch, *Amaretto*, Frangelico, crème de cacao, crème de banana, Irish cream liqueur, Kahlúa)

1. Combine cream and chocolate in a heavy 1-quart saucepan. Stir over very low heat to melt chocolate. When mixture is smooth and the chocolate is melted, stir in liquor. (This can be done up to 4 hours ahead. Reheat over very low heat or in a microwave.)

2. Transfer fondue to a fondue pot or other pot with a heat source, and serve with hulled strawberries (halved if large), banana chunks, clementine segments, apple slices, donut holes, waffle squares, butter cookies, angel food cake cubes, cake cubes, brownie cubes, biscotti, or sugar cookies.

Variation: If you're serving the fondue to children or adults who cannot tolerate alcohol, you can substitute ¼ to ½ teaspoon pure extract for the liquor or liqueur.

Dip-Tionary

Amaretto is a liqueur that has the flavor of almonds but it is frequently distilled from the kernels of apricot pits as well. It was invented in Saronno, Italy, but now many are made in the United States.

Bittersweet Chocolate Coconut Cream Fondue

| Serves: **6** | Prep time: **10 minutes** | Cook time: **5 minutes** |

9 oz. bittersweet chocolate, chopped

1 oz. unsweetened chocolate, chopped

1 cup sweetened cream of coconut (such as Coco López)

$\frac{1}{2}$ cup heavy cream

$\frac{1}{4}$ cup dark rum

$\frac{1}{4}$ tsp. pure coconut extract

1. Combine bittersweet chocolate, unsweetened chocolate, cream of coconut, and cream in a heavy 1-quart saucepan. Stir over very low heat to melt chocolate. When mixture is smooth and chocolate is melted, stir in rum and coconut extract. (This can be done up to 4 hours ahead. Reheat over very low heat or in a microwave.)

Fon-Don'ts

Be sure you only use pure extracts in cooking. They may cost a bit more, but you only use them in minute quantities, and they last for up to 2 years after they're opened. The flavor of extracts is intense, and the chemical taste from artificial extracts is unpleasant.

2. Transfer fondue to a fondue pot or other pot with a heat source, and serve with hulled strawberries (halved if large), banana chunks, clementine segments, apple slices, dried coconut slices, dried apricots, crystallized ginger, donut holes, waffle squares, butter cookies, angel food cake cubes, cake cubes, brownie cubes, coconut macaroons, or sugar cookies.

Mexican Chocolate Fondue

| Serves: **6** | Prep time: **15 minutes** | Cook time: **5 minutes** |

$\frac{1}{2}$ cup sliced almonds
$\frac{1}{2}$ cup heavy cream
10 oz. bittersweet chocolate, chopped

$\frac{1}{2}$ tsp. ground cinnamon
3 TB. amaretto
$\frac{1}{4}$ tsp. pure almond extract

1. Toast almonds in a 350°F oven for 5 to 7 minutes or until lightly browned. Chop and set aside.

2. Combine cream, chocolate, and cinnamon in a heavy 1-quart saucepan. Stir over very low heat to melt chocolate. When mixture is smooth and chocolate is melted, stir in almonds, amaretto, and almond extract. (This can be done up to 4 hours ahead. Reheat over very low heat or in a microwave.)

3. Transfer fondue to a fondue pot or other pot with a heat source, and serve with hulled strawberries (halved if large), banana chunks, clementine segments, apple slices, donut holes, waffle squares, butter cookies, angel food cake cubes, spice cake cubes, brownie cubes, biscotti, or sugar cookies.

Fondue Facts

The Aztecs first discovered chocolate, and our word comes from the Aztec *xocolatl*, which means "bitter water." Famed King Montezuma believed chocolate was an aphrodisiac and is reported to have consumed some 50 cups a day.

Spiced Chocolate Fondue

| Serves: **6** | Prep time: **10 minutes** | Cook time: **5 minutes** |

½ cup sour cream
10 oz. bittersweet chocolate, chopped

½ tsp. Chinese five-spice powder
Pinch cayenne
3 TB. Cognac or brandy

1. Combine sour cream, chocolate, Chinese five-spice powder, and cayenne in a heavy 1-quart saucepan. Stir over very low heat to melt chocolate. When mixture is smooth and chocolate is melted, stir in Cognac. (This can be done up to 4 hours ahead. Reheat over very low heat or in a microwave.)

Dip Tips

It might seem odd to see cayenne listed as an ingredient in a dessert recipe, but a tiny amount of a spicy flavor enhances the taste buds' ability to appreciate sweet flavor. Many European desserts call for a grind or two of fresh black pepper for the same reason.

2. Transfer fondue to a fondue pot or other pot with a heat source, and serve with hulled strawberries (halved if large), banana chunks, clementine segments, apple slices, donut holes, waffle squares, butter cookies, French toast slices, cake cubes, gingerbread cubes, biscotti, or sugar cookies.

Milk Chocolate Peanut Butter Fondue

| Serves: **6** | Prep time: **10 minutes** | Cook time: **5 minutes** |

¹/₂ cup heavy cream
10 oz. milk chocolate, chopped

¹/₂ cup crunchy peanut butter
1 TB. Frangelico

1. Combine cream, chocolate, and peanut butter in a heavy 1-quart sauce-pan. Stir over very low heat to melt chocolate. When mixture is smooth and chocolate is melted, stir in Frangelico. (This can be done up to 4 hours ahead. Reheat over very low heat or in a microwave.)

2. Transfer fondue to a fondue pot or other pot with a heat source, and serve with hulled strawberries (halved if large), banana chunks, clementine segments, apple slices, donut holes, waffle squares, butter cookies, angel food cake cubes, cake cubes, brownie cubes, biscotti, or sugar cookies.

Fon-Don'ts

You might think a natural peanut butter would be better than one with sugar, but in this case, it isn't. If you want to use a ground nut butter, check the sugar level and keep adding sugar until it tastes like commercial peanut butter. This *is* a dessert, remember!

Milk Chocolate Toffee Fondue

| Serves: **6** | Prep time: **10 minutes** | Cook time: **5 minutes** |

$^1\!/_2$ cup heavy cream
10 oz. milk chocolate, chopped

$^1\!/_2$ *toffee* bits
1 TB. crème de cacao

1. Combine cream and chocolate in a heavy 1-quart saucepan. Stir over very low heat to melt chocolate. When mixture is smooth and chocolate is melted, stir in toffee bits and crème de cacao. (This can be done up to 4 hours ahead. Reheat over very low heat or in a microwave.)

2. Transfer fondue to a fondue pot or other pot with a heat source, and serve with hulled strawberries (halved if large), banana chunks, clementine segments, apple slices, donut holes, waffle squares, butter cookies, angel food cake cubes, cake cubes, brownie cubes, biscotti, or sugar cookies.

Dip-Tionary

Toffee is a candy made by cooking sugar with water and usually butter until it's browned. On a candy thermometer, the temperature should reach between 260° and 300°F.

Variation: If you can't find toffee bits, you can always break up hard caramel candies or a nut brittle.

Chocolate Raspberry Fondue

| Serves: **6** | Prep time: **10 minutes** | Cook time: **5 minutes** |

½ cup heavy cream
¼ cup raspberry preserves

10 oz. bittersweet chocolate, chopped
3 TB. Chambord *liqueur*

1. Combine cream, preserves, and chocolate in a heavy 1-quart saucepan. Stir over very low heat to melt chocolate. When mixture is smooth and chocolate is melted, stir in Chambord. (This can be done up to 4 hours ahead. Reheat over very low heat or in a microwave.)

2. Transfer fondue to a fondue pot or other pot with a heat source, and serve with hulled strawberries (halved if large), banana chunks, clementine segments, apple slices, donut holes, waffle squares, butter cookies, angel food cake cubes, cake cubes, brownie cubes, biscotti, or sugar cookies.

Dip-Tionary

Liqueur is the general name for a strongly flavored, sweet alcoholic beverage made by infusing grain alcohol or a spirit such as rum or brandy with flavoring, such as fruits, nuts, herbs, or spices.

Chocolate Espresso Fondue

| Serves: **6** | Prep time: **15 minutes** | Cook time: **5 minutes** |

¼ cup water
2 TB. instant espresso powder
½ cup heavy cream

10 oz. bittersweet chocolate, chopped
2 TB. Kahlúa or other coffee-flavored liqueur

1. Combine water and espresso powder in a heavy 1-quart saucepan. Bring to a boil over high heat, and stir to dissolve powder. Reduce heat to low, and stir in cream and chocolate. Stir over very low heat to melt chocolate. When mixture is smooth and chocolate is melted, stir in Kahlúa. (This can be done up to 4 hours ahead. Reheat over very low heat or in a microwave.)

Fondue Facts

Italians drink more than 9 billion cups a year. What differentiates espresso from other strong coffee is that it is brewed by forcing hot water under high pressure through finely ground coffee. It was invented in Naples in 1901.

2. Transfer fondue to a fondue pot or other pot with a heat source, and serve with hulled strawberries (halved if large), banana chunks, clementine segments, apple slices, donut holes, waffle squares, butter cookies, angel food cake cubes, cake cubes, brownie cubes, biscotti, or sugar cookies.

White Chocolate Maple Walnut Fondue

| Serves: **6** | Prep time: **15 minutes** | Cook time: **5 minutes** |

$\frac{1}{2}$ cup chopped walnuts
$\frac{1}{3}$ cup heavy cream
$\frac{1}{3}$ cup pure maple syrup
10 oz. white chocolate, chopped

1 TB. bourbon
1 tsp. pure maple extract
$\frac{1}{4}$ tsp. walnut extract

1. Toast walnuts in a 350°F oven for 5 to 7 minutes or until lightly browned. Set aside.

2. Combine cream, maple syrup, and chocolate in a heavy 1-quart saucepan. Stir over very low heat to melt chocolate. When mixture is smooth and chocolate is melted, stir in walnuts, bourbon, maple extract, and walnut extract. (This can be done up to 4 hours ahead. Reheat over very low heat or in a microwave.)

3. Transfer fondue to a fondue pot or other pot with a heat source, and serve with hulled strawberries (halved if large), banana chunks, clementine segments, apple slices, donut holes, waffle squares, butter cookies, angel food cake cubes, cake cubes, brownie cubes, biscotti, or sugar cookies.

Dip Tips

It makes all the difference to the flavor of this fondue or any dish to use only pure maple syrup and not artificially flavored pancake syrup. The pure stuff is in nearly every supermarket today, so there's no excuse for using the artificial stuff!

White Chocolate Cranberry Orange Fondue

Serves: **6**	*Prep time:* **15 minutes**	*Cook time:* **15 minutes**

1 cup freshly squeezed orange juice
¹/₂ cup heavy cream
10 oz. white chocolate, chopped

1 TB. grated orange *zest*
¹/₂ cup dried cranberries, coarsely chopped
2 TB. triple sec or other orange-flavored liqueur

1. Place orange juice in a heavy 1-quart saucepan. Bring to a boil over high heat and cook, stirring occasionally, 10 minutes or until liquid is reduced by ³/₄. Add cream, chocolate, and orange zest, and reduce heat to very low. Stir over very low heat to melt chocolate. When mixture is smooth and chocolate is melted, stir in dried cranberries and liqueur. (This can be done up to 4 hours ahead. Reheat over very low heat or in a microwave.)

Dip-Tionary

Zest is the outermost layer of the skin of citrus fruits that contains the fruit's precious aromatic oils. You can remove the zest with a citrus zester, or you can grate it off with the small side of a box grater.

2. Transfer fondue to a fondue pot or other pot with a heat source, and serve with hulled strawberries (halved if large), banana chunks, clementine segments, apple slices, donut holes, waffle squares, butter cookies, angel food cake cubes, cake cubes, brownie cubes, biscotti, or sugar cookies.

White Chocolate Mint Fondue

| Serves: **6** | Prep time: **10 minutes** | Cook time: **5 minutes** |

½ cup heavy cream
10 oz. white chocolate, chopped

2 TB. finely chopped fresh peppermint leaves
¼ cup crème de menthe

1. Combine cream and chocolate in a heavy 1-quart saucepan. Stir over very low heat to melt chocolate. When mixture is smooth and chocolate is melted, stir in chopped peppermint and crème de menthe. (This can be done up to 4 hours ahead. Reheat over very low heat or in a microwave.)

2. Transfer fondue to a fondue pot or other pot with a heat source, and serve with hulled strawberries (halved if large), banana chunks, clementine segments, apple slices, donut holes, waffle squares, butter cookies, angel food cake cubes, cake cubes, brownie cubes, biscotti, or sugar cookies.

Dip Tips

Peppermint and spearmint are two types of mint widely available. Peppermint has bright green leaves and a more pungent flavor; spearmint is more gray-green and milder. If you're using spearmint in place of peppermint, add an extra sprig to make up the difference in flavor.

Chapter 13

Sweet Sensations

In This Chapter

- ◆ Caramel- and butterscotch-based fondues
- ◆ Nutty fondues
- ◆ Fondues inspired by international desserts

Just think of all the toppings you find in an ice-cream bar. Flavors such as caramel and butterscotch come to mind, along with crunchy nuts. Those same flavors work wonderfully as fondues. There's a whole world of fabulous flavors in the dessert spectrum beyond chocolate, and those are the recipes you'll find in this chapter. (Need a chocolate fix? Turn back to Chapter 12.)

Other recipes in this chapter are combinations found in baked goods. You're enjoying them in a warm liquid form!

Caramel Chemistry

Caramel is simply sugar and water cooked to a high temperature. But the change from simple sugar syrup to caramel is hardly a simple one. The sugar melts and thickens into a syrup that slowly begins to change color from light yellow to deep mahogany brown.

The sugar breaks down from a single species of molecule to recombine to form at least 100 different reaction products, among them sour organic acids, sweet and bitter derivatives, and brown-colored polymers. This change becomes noticeable from 320°F to 360°F because large amounts of energy are required to start the molecular changes. As the temperature of the syrup rises, there's no more moisture left to evaporate, and the color deepens. At about 340°F, the syrup can be called caramel.

The easiest way to judge the temperature of a sugar syrup is by using a candy or deep-fry thermometer. Place it in the middle of the pan—and not on the bottom of the pot where the temperature will be higher.

But long before there were such thermometers, cooks judged the progress of a syrup by dropping drips into a cup of ice water and gauging the results. Here are the clues:

♦ The "soft ball" stage is between 235°F and 250°F. When you place a few drops of syrup in the water, you can pick it up between your fingers and it feels soft.

♦ The "hard ball" stage is the middle point before you get caramel. It's between 250°F and 275°F, and a drop of the syrup forms a hard ball in the water.

Successful Serving

A variety of fruits and pastries for dipping are part of the fun of a dessert fondue. That's why I give you so many suggestions with each recipe. If you have one or two fruits and one or two pastry products, all your diners will be thrilled.

The recipes in this chapter also lend themselves to augmenting the fondue with a crunchy dip. Place bowls of crushed cookies, chopped nuts, or toasted coconut on the table so diners can take a second dip into the crunchy topping. The fondue will adhere it to the dipped food.

Caramel Rum Fondue

| Serves: **6** | Prep time: **5 minutes** | Cook time: **15 minutes** |

2 cups granulated sugar
¹/₂ cup water
¹/₄ lb. (1 stick) unsalted butter,
softened and cut into small pieces

2 cups heavy cream
¹/₄ cup rum
1 tsp. pure vanilla extract

1. Combine sugar and water in a heavy 1-quart saucepan. Bring to a simmer over medium heat, swirling occasionally. Cover the pan, raise the heat to medium-high, and cook until liquid gives off large, thick bubbles. Uncover the pan, and cook until syrup reaches a golden brown.

2. Remove the pan from the heat, and stir in butter with a long-handled wooden spoon. Add cream, stirring constantly, and then add rum and vanilla extract. Return the pan to low heat, and stir constantly until lumps have melted and syrup is smooth.

3. Transfer fondue to a fondue pot or other pot with a heat source, and serve with hulled strawberries (halved if large), banana chunks, clementine segments, apple slices, dried apricots, crystallized ginger, donut holes, waffle squares, angel food cake cubes, pound cake cubes, brownie cubes, coconut macaroons, or sugar cookies.

Dip Tips

To clean the pan in which the caramel was made, fill it with water to the top of the hardened caramel and place over a flame. Stir it as the water comes to a boil, and the pan will be virtually clean.

Variation: Any flavor of liquor or liqueur can be used in place of the rum. For inspiration, consult the note in Chapter 12 on flavorings for chocolate fondue.

Caramel Cheese Fondue

Serves: 6 | **Prep time: 10 minutes** | **Cook time: 5 minutes**

6 oz. (2 cups) candy caramels,
unwrapped

³/₄ cup heavy cream

1 (8-oz.) pkg. cream cheese,
softened

1 tsp. pure vanilla extract

1. Combine caramels and cream in a heavy 1-quart saucepan. Cook over low heat, stirring occasionally, until caramels are melted and cream comes to a simmer.

2. Whisk in cream cheese, and cook, stirring occasionally, until smooth and bubbly. Stir in vanilla extract.

3. Transfer fondue to a fondue pot or other pot with a heat source, and serve with hulled strawberries (halved if large), banana chunks, apple slices, dried coconut slices, dried apricots, donut holes, waffle squares, butter cookies, angel food cake cubes, pound cake cubes, brownie cubes, or sugar cookies.

Fon-Don'ts

Cooking over low heat doesn't mean you can ignore the pan. You've got to watch cream carefully when cooking with it. In a recipe like this one, the cream can boil over the pan and the caramels can scorch if you don't stir it occasionally.

Creamy Butterscotch Fondue

Serves: 6 | *Prep time:* **5 minutes** | *Cook time:* **15 minutes**

2 cups firmly packed light brown sugar	6 TB. unsalted butter
1 cup light corn syrup	1½ cups heavy cream
	1 tsp. pure vanilla extract

1. Combine brown sugar, corn syrup, butter, and 1 cup the cream in a heavy 1-quart saucepan. Bring to a boil over medium heat, stirring frequently. Reduce the heat to medium-low, and cook syrup without stirring for 5 to 10 minutes or until it reaches 234°F on a candy thermometer or creates a soft ball when dropped into a cup of ice water.

2. Remove the pan from the heat, and stir in remaining ½ cup cream and vanilla extract.

3. Transfer fondue to a fondue pot or other pot with a heat source, and serve with hulled strawberries (halved if large), banana chunks, clementine segments, apple slices, slices of dried coconut, dried apricots, crystallized ginger, donut holes, waffle squares, butter cookies, angel food cake cubes, pound cake cubes, brownie cubes, coconut macaroons, or sugar cookies.

Fon-Don'ts

When you're making butterscotch or caramel, don't cook the syrup to the color you think it should be or it might be too dark. Take the pan off the flame when the liquid's not quite as dark as you would like it. It will continue to darken from the heat in the pan.

Easy Mexican *Dulce de Leche* Fondue

Serves: 6 | **Prep time: 5 minutes** | **Cook time: 2¹/₂ hours**

3 (14-oz.) cans sweetened condensed milk

¹/₄ cup dark rum

1 tsp. pure vanilla extract, preferably Mexican

1. Remove the labels from the cans, stand the cans in a deep stock pot, and fill the pot with hot water. Cover the pan, and bring to a boil over high heat. Reduce the heat to low, and allow the cans to simmer gently for 2¹/₂ hours. Add water as necessary to keep the cans covered. *It is imperative that the cans are covered with water at all times or they could explode.*

2. Remove the cans from the water with tongs and allow them to cool. Pour the cans' contents into a fondue pot or other pot with a heat source, and stir in rum and vanilla extract.

3. Serve with hulled strawberries (halved if large), banana chunks, apple slices, dried coconut slices, dried apricots, crystallized ginger, donut holes, waffle squares, butter cookies, pound cake cubes, brownie cubes, coconut macaroons, or sugar cookies.

Variation: You can use pure almond extract in place of the vanilla. You can also add chopped toasted almonds to the fondue.

Fondue Facts

Dulce de leche means "sweet milk" in Spanish, and it's popular in all Hispanic countries. It's sometimes called *cajeta*, and it's used as a spread, dip, or topping. This easy method is how it's made in the Yucatan province of Mexico.

Crystallized Ginger Mascarpone Fondue

| Serves: **6** | Prep time: **10 minutes** | Cook time: **10 minutes** |

1 lb. (2 cups) *mascarpone* cheese
¹/₂ cup heavy cream
¹/₂ cup confectioners' sugar
¹/₄ cup finely chopped crystallized ginger

1 tsp. grated lemon zest
2 tsp. cornstarch
¹/₂ tsp. pure vanilla extract

1. Combine mascarpone, ¹/₄ cup cream, confectioners' sugar, ginger, and lemon zest in a heavy 1-quart saucepan. Stir until smooth, and bring to a boil over low heat, stirring occasionally.

2. Combine remaining ¹/₄ cup cream and cornstarch in a small bowl, and stir to dissolve cornstarch. Add to fondue, and bring to a simmer, stirring constantly. Cook over low heat for 1 to 2 minutes or until fondue has thickened. Stir in vanilla extract.

3. Transfer fondue to a fondue pot or other pot with a heat source, and serve with hulled strawberries (halved if large), banana chunks, clementine segments, dried coconut slices, dried apricots, donut holes, waffle squares, pound cake cubes, brownie cubes, coconut macaroons, or sugar cookies.

Dip-Tionary

Mascarpone is a rich double or triple cream cheese made from milk and famous in the Lombardy region of Italy. It resembles cream cheese but has a far higher butter content. If you can't find any, use half cream cheese and half unsalted butter instead.

Variation: You can substitute ¹/₂ cup finely chopped dried apricots for the crystallized ginger. Soak them in ¹/₂ cup boiling water for 10 minutes before adding them.

Ricotta Orange Fondue

| Serves: **6** | Prep time: **10 minutes** | Cook time: **10 minutes** |

1½ cups crème fraîche
1 cup heavy cream
³/₄ cup confectioners' sugar
¹/₄ cup triple sec or other clear
orange liqueur

1 TB. grated orange zest
2 tsp. cornstarch
12 oz. whole milk ricotta cheese

1. Combine crème fraîche, ³/₄ cup cream, sugar, triple sec, and orange zest in a heavy 1-quart saucepan. Stir until smooth, and bring to a boil over low heat, stirring occasionally.

2. Combine remaining ¹/₄ cup cream and cornstarch in a small bowl, and stir to dissolve cornstarch. Add to fondue, and bring to a simmer, stirring constantly. Cook over low heat for 1 to 2 minutes or until fondue has thickened. Whisk in ricotta cheese until smooth and bubbly again.

3. Transfer fondue to a fondue pot or other pot with a heat source, and serve with hulled strawberries (halved if large), clementine segments, apple slices, dried apricots, donut holes, waffle squares, butter cookies, angel food cake cubes, pound cake cubes, coconut macaroons, or sugar cookies.

Variation: This delicate white fondue takes well to any number of different flavors. Use a liqueur that's clear rather than colored, so kirsch, white crème de cacao, or white crème de menthe all work well. Omit the orange zest if you're not using triple sec.

Fon-Don'ts

Crème fraîche and sour cream may look the same and have a similar flavor, but don't ever substitute sour cream in a recipe that's cooked. The crème fraîche becomes creamy when heated, but sour cream curdles if it's allowed to come to a boil.

Peanut Butter Fondue

Serves: 6 | **Prep time: 10 minutes** | **Cook time: 10 minutes**

½ cup heavy cream

¼ cup firmly packed light brown sugar

4 TB. unsalted butter, cut into pieces

½ cup smooth or chunky peanut butter

⅓ cup marshmallow cream

½ tsp. pure vanilla extract

1. Combine cream, brown sugar, and butter in a heavy 1-quart saucepan. Bring to a boil over medium heat, stirring frequently.

2. Whisk in peanut butter and marshmallow cream. Continue to cook until mixture begins to bubble. Whisk in vanilla extract.

3. Transfer fondue to a fondue pot or other pot with a heat source, and serve with hulled strawberries (halved if large), banana chunks, apple slices, donut holes, waffle squares, butter cookies, pound cake cubes, brownie cubes, or sugar cookies.

Tiramisu Fondue

| Serves: **6** | Prep time: **10 minutes** | Cook time: **10 minutes** |

$^2/_3$ cup heavy cream
1 lb. (2 cups) mascarpone
$^1/_2$ cup confectioners' sugar
$^1/_4$ cup sweet Marsala wine

1 TB. instant espresso powder
1 TB. unsweetened cocoa
4 large egg yolks
$^1/_2$ tsp. pure vanilla extract

1. Combine $^1/_3$ cup cream, mascarpone, sugar, Marsala, espresso powder, and cocoa the in the top of a double boiler set over simmering water. Heat to a simmer, whisking mixture until smooth.

2. Whisk egg yolks with remaining $^1/_3$ cup cream in a mixing bowl. Slowly whisk $^1/_2$ cup hot mixture into egg yolks and then pour egg mixture into the double boiler. Reduce the heat to low, and cook, stirring constantly, until mixture thickens and coats the back of a spoon. Do not let mixture boil. Stir in vanilla extract.

3. Transfer fondue to a fondue pot or other pot with a heat source, and serve with hulled strawberries (halved if large), peach slices, Italian ladyfingers, biscotti, donut holes, angel food cake cubes, pound cake cubes, or sugar cookies.

Fondue Facts

Tiramisu literally means "pick me up" in Italian because it contains espresso and cocoa, two ingredients containing caffeine. This dessert made with mascarpone custard and espresso was born at the El Toulè restaurant in Treviso in the 1960s.

Chapter 14

Fabulous and Fruity

In This Chapter

- ◆ Luscious, fruity fondues
- ◆ Fondue versions of desserts and drinks
- ◆ Fruity fondues—fast!

If you're excited to see strawberry shortcake on a dessert menu or piña colada as a featured cocktail, the recipes in this chapter are for you. All these fondues star the contents of the fruit section, and many of them are warm liquid forms of other favorite drinks and desserts.

It's important to log in approximately nine servings of fruit and vegetables a day, and what could be a more delicious way than with dessert? Fruit fondues please crowds of all ages, and most of them are somewhat lighter than other dessert fondues.

Fruit Forms

Many of the recipes in this chapter specify that the fruit used remains raw. But using fruit that's already been processed in some way can save a lot of time, so you'll find recipes that take advantage of this convenience here, too.

For example, unsweetened applesauce is nothing more than pre-cooked apples, so it only makes sense to save the time and energy needed to make it from scratch. It's also time-consuming to peel peaches; they have to be dropped into boiling water for 30 seconds and then peeled or the peel will be unpleasant in the fondue.

Dry-pack frozen fruits are a boon, so I've listed them as an alternative in many of these recipes. They're always picked and frozen at the peak of ripeness, so if a fresh fruit isn't in season locally, you'll probably get better flavor from frozen fruits. And you can't beat the convenience.

Cinnamon Apple Fondue

| Serves: **6** | Prep time: **5 minutes** | Cook time: **5 minutes** |

4 TB. unsalted butter
$^1/_4$ cup all-purpose flour
$^1/_2$ cup heavy cream

$1^1/_2$ cups unsweetened applesauce
$^3/_4$ tsp. ground cinnamon

1. Melt butter in a heavy 1-quart saucepan over medium heat. Reduce the heat to low, add flour, and cook for 2 minutes, stirring constantly.

2. Raise the heat to medium, and whisk in cream, applesauce, and cinnamon. Bring to a boil, whisking until smooth.

3. Transfer fondue to a fondue pot or other pot with a heat source, and serve with hulled strawberries (halved if large), apple slices, crystallized ginger, donut holes, waffle squares, angel food cake cubes, pound cake cubes, brownie cubes, coconut macaroons, or sugar cookies.

Fondue Facts

There isn't really a Jolly Green Giant, but there certainly was a Johnny Appleseed. Named John Chapman, he was born in Massachusetts in 1774. Unlike the artistic depictions of him propagating apples by tossing seeds out of his backpack, Chapman actually started nurseries in the Allegheny Valley in 1800. By the time of his death in 1845, he had pushed as far west as Indiana, establishing groves of apple trees.

Lemon Curd Mascarpone Fondue

| Serves: **6** | Prep time: **15 minutes** | Cook time: **10 minutes** |

3 large eggs
½ cup granulated sugar
⅔ cup freshly squeezed lemon juice
1 TB. grated lemon zest

6 TB. unsalted butter, cut into ¼-inch dice
1 TB. cornstarch
½ cup mascarpone

1. Combine eggs and sugar in a heavy 1-quart saucepan, and whisk until thick and lemon colored. Add ½ cup lemon juice, lemon zest, and butter. Place the pan over medium-low heat, and cook, whisking frequently, for 5 to 6 minutes or until *curd* is thick and small bubbles begin to appear on the surface.

2. Combine remaining lemon juice and cornstarch in a small bowl, and stir to dissolve cornstarch. Add to fondue, and bring to a simmer, stirring constantly. Cook over low heat for 1 to 2 minutes or until fondue has thickened. Remove the pan from the heat, and whisk in mascarpone.

3. Transfer fondue to a fondue pot or other pot with a heat source, and serve with hulled strawberries (halved if large), clementine segments, donut holes, waffle squares, angel food cake cubes, pound cake cubes, coconut macaroons, or sugar cookies.

Variation: Substitute lime juice and lime zest for the lemon juice and zest.

Dip-Tionary

Curd is most often refers to cheese i.e., separating the curd from the liquid whey, but it is also the name of a family of thick fruit spreads, especially popular in England, made from sugar, butter, fruit juice, and eggs. When the curd is cool, it's spread on breakfast pastries.

Bananas Foster Fondue

Serves: **6**	Prep time: **10 minutes**	Cook time: **10 minutes**

2 ripe bananas
$\frac{1}{2}$ cup heavy cream
4 TB. unsalted butter

$\frac{1}{2}$ cup firmly packed dark brown sugar
$\frac{1}{4}$ cup crème de banana
2 tsp. cornstarch

1. Place bananas and cream in a food processor fitted with a steel blade or in a blender. Purée until smooth, and set aside.

2. Melt butter in a heavy 1-quart saucepan over medium heat, and add brown sugar. Cook for 3 minutes, stirring occasionally. Add banana purée, and bring to a boil over medium heat, stirring occasionally. Reduce the heat to low, and simmer for 3 minutes, stirring occasionally.

3. Combine crème de banana and cornstarch in a small bowl, and stir to dissolve cornstarch. Add to fondue, and bring to a simmer, stirring constantly. Cook over low heat for 1 to 2 minutes or until fondue has thickened.

Fondue Facts

Bananas Foster is the signature dish of Brennan's Restaurant in New Orleans, known for its fabulous breakfasts. The dish was developed in the 1950s and named for Richard Foster, a regular customer.

4. Transfer fondue to a fondue pot or other pot with a heat source, and serve with hulled strawberries (halved if large), donut holes, waffle squares, butter cookies, angel food cake cubes, pound cake cubes, brownie cubes, coconut macaroons, or sugar cookies.

Raspberry Fondue

| *Serves:* **6** | *Prep time:* **5 minutes** | *Cook time:* **15 minutes** |

4 (6-oz.) containers fresh raspberries, rinsed, or 24 oz. (3 cups) dry-pack frozen raspberries, thawed

$\frac{1}{2}$ cup red wine

$\frac{1}{4}$ cup raspberry preserves

$\frac{1}{2}$ cup granulated sugar

2 TB. water

1 TB. freshly squeezed lemon juice

2 TB. cornstarch

1. Place raspberries, wine, raspberry preserves, and sugar in a food processor fitted with a steel blade or in a blender. Purée until smooth.

2. Scrape mixture into a heavy 1-quart saucepan, and bring to a boil over medium heat, stirring occasionally. Reduce the heat to low, and simmer mixture for 5 minutes, stirring occasionally.

3. Combine water, lemon juice, and cornstarch in a small bowl, and stir to dissolve cornstarch. Add to fondue, and bring to a simmer, stirring constantly. Cook over low heat for 1 to 2 minutes or until fondue has thickened.

4. Transfer fondue to a fondue pot or other pot with a heat source, and serve with dried apricots, crystallized ginger, donut holes, waffle squares, angel food cake cubes, pound cake cubes, brownie cubes, or sugar cookies.

Variation: Substitute strawberries, blueberries, or blackberries and their appropriate jam for the raspberries.

Dip Tips

This recipe doesn't require you to strain out the raspberry seeds simply because I'm not bothered by them. If you are, here's a way to strain any berry purée: put the purée in a wire mesh strainer and rub it with a rubber spatula. You'll get all the juice through, and the seeds will remain in the strainer.

Cherries Jubilee Fondue

Serves: 6 | Prep time: **10 minutes** | Cook time: **10 minutes**

1 (14-oz.) can sour cherries, drained with syrup reserved, and coarsely chopped
$\frac{1}{2}$ cup cherry preserves
$\frac{1}{4}$ cup granulated sugar

1 TB. freshly squeezed lemon juice
2 TB. kirsch
2 tsp. cornstarch

1. Combine cherries, reserved juice, cherry preserves, sugar, and lemon juice in a heavy 1-quart saucepan. Bring to a boil over medium heat, stirring occasionally. Reduce the heat to low, and simmer for 3 minutes.

2. Combine kirsch and cornstarch in a small bowl, and stir to dissolve cornstarch. Add to fondue, and bring to a simmer, stirring constantly. Cook over low heat for 1 to 2 minutes, or until fondue has thickened.

3. Transfer fondue to a fondue pot or other pot with a heat source, and serve with hulled strawberries (halved if large), apple slices, dried apricots, donut holes, angel food cake cubes, pound cake cubes, brownie cubes, coconut macaroons, or sugar cookies.

Fon-Don'ts

Right next to the cans of sour cherries—which might show a cherry pie on the label—are cans of cherry pie filling. Be sure you don't pick up the cherry pie filling by mistake.

Coconut Mango Fondue

| Serves: **6** | Prep time: **10 minutes** | Cook time: **10 minutes** |

2 ripe mangoes, peeled and finely chopped

1 cup sweetened cream of coconut (such as Coco López)

$\frac{1}{2}$ cup heavy cream

$\frac{1}{4}$ cup dark rum

1 tsp. grated lime zest

$\frac{1}{4}$ tsp. pure coconut extract

2 TB. freshly squeezed lime juice

2 tsp. cornstarch

1. Combine mangoes, cream of coconut, cream, rum, lime zest, and coconut extract in a heavy 1-quart saucepan. Bring to a boil over medium heat, stirring occasionally. Reduce the heat to low, and simmer mixture for 5 minutes, stirring occasionally.

2. Combine lime juice and cornstarch in a small bowl, and stir to dissolve cornstarch. Add to fondue, and bring to a simmer, stirring constantly. Cook over low heat for 1 to 2 minutes or until fondue has thickened.

Fondue Facts

Mangoes are called "the apples of the tropics" because they're the most widely grown fruits in the world. Famed Impressionist Paul Gauguin made them the subject of a work from his Tahitian period.

3. Transfer fondue to a fondue pot or other pot with a heat source, and serve with hulled strawberries (halved if large), banana chunks, clementine segments, dried coconut slices, crystallized ginger, donut holes, angel food cake cubes, pound cake cubes, coconut macaroons, or sugar cookies.

Peach Melba Fondue

| Serves: **6** | Prep time: **10 minutes** | Cook time: **10 minutes** |

2½ cups peach slices (either 3 ripe peaches, peeled and sliced, or frozen peach slices, thawed)

1 cup peach nectar

¼ cup raspberry jam

3 TB. Chambord liqueur

1 TB. freshly squeezed lemon juice

1 TB. cornstarch

1. Combine peach slices, peach nectar, and raspberry jam in a heavy 1-quart saucepan. Bring to a boil over medium heat, stirring occasionally. Reduce the heat to low, and simmer mixture for 5 minutes, stirring occasionally. Transfer mixture to a food processor fitted with a steel blade or a blender. Purée until smooth, and return it to the pan.

2. Combine Chambord, lemon juice, and cornstarch in a small bowl, and stir to dissolve cornstarch. Add to fondue, and bring to a simmer, stirring constantly. Cook over low heat for 1 to 2 minutes or until fondue has thickened.

3. Transfer fondue to a fondue pot or other pot with a heat source, and serve with hulled strawberries (halved if large), donut holes, waffle squares, angel food cake cubes, pound cake cubes, coconut macaroons, or sugar cookies.

Fondue Facts_____

Pêche Melba was created by famed French chef Auguste Escoffier in the late 1800s in honor of Dame Nellie Melba, a popular Australian opera singer in Paris at the time. We might not remember her as a singer, but she was immortalized as a classic dessert.

Piña Colada Fondue

| Serves: **6** | Prep time: **10 minutes** | Cook time: **10 minutes** |

2 cups diced fresh pineapple or 2 cups crushed pineapple packed in pineapple juice, drained
1 cup sweetened cream of coconut (such as Coco López)

$^1/_2$ cup rum
1 TB. freshly squeezed lime juice
1 TB. cornstarch

1. Place 1 cup pineapple in a food processor fitted with a steel blade or in a blender. Purée until smooth. Finely chop remaining 1 cup pineapple.

2. Combine all pineapple, cream of coconut, and rum in a heavy 1-quart saucepan. Bring to a boil over medium heat, stirring occasionally. Reduce the heat to low, and simmer mixture for 5 minutes, stirring occasionally.

3. Combine lime juice and cornstarch in a small bowl, and stir to dissolve cornstarch. Add to fondue, and bring to a simmer, stirring constantly. Cook over low heat for 1 to 2 minutes or until fondue has thickened.

Dip Tips

A small amount of lemon juice or lime juice is frequently added to dessert recipes to boost the flavor of the other fruits. You won't taste the lime juice in this small a quantity, but its presence will make you taste the coconut and pineapple more.

4. Transfer fondue to a fondue pot or other pot with a heat source, and serve with hulled strawberries (halved if large), banana chunks, clementine segments, dried coconut slices, crystallized ginger, donut holes, angel food cake cubes, pound cake cubes, coconut macaroons, or sugar cookies.

Totally Apricot Fondue

Serves: **6**	Prep time: **10 minutes**	Cook time: **10 minutes**

4 (4-oz.) jars strained apricot baby food

¹/₂ cup finely chopped dried apricots

¹/₂ cup apricot nectar

¹/₂ cup heavy cream

3 TB. apricot brandy

1 TB. cornstarch

1. Combine strained apricot baby food, dried apricots, apricot nectar, and cream in a heavy 1-quart saucepan. Bring to a boil over medium heat, stirring occasionally. Reduce the heat to low, and simmer mixture for 5 minutes, stirring occasionally.

2. Combine apricot brandy and cornstarch in a small bowl, and stir to dissolve cornstarch. Add to fondue, and bring to a simmer, stirring constantly. Cook over low heat for 1 to 2 minutes or until fondue has thickened.

3. Transfer fondue to a fondue pot or other pot with a heat source, and serve with hulled strawberries (halved if large), clementine segments, donut holes, waffle squares, angel food cake cubes, pound cake cubes, or sugar cookies.

Fon-Don'ts

Be careful when shopping for strained fruit in the baby food aisle if you, like me, are rather foreign to that part of the supermarket. Some baby food contains cereal and other ingredients, and that's not what you want.

Variation: Peaches also come in strained, dried, and nectar forms, and the amounts of these will make this a Totally Peach Fondue.

Appendix A

Glossary

all-purpose flour   Flour that contains only the inner part of the wheat grain. Usable for all purposes from cakes to gravies.

allspice   Named for its flavor echoes of several spices (cinnamon, cloves, nutmeg), allspice is used in many desserts and in rich marinades and stews.

almonds   Mild, sweet, and crunchy nuts that combine nicely with creamy and sweet food items.

amaretto   A popular almond liqueur.

applejack   A brandy distilled from apple cider.

basil   A flavorful, almost sweet, resinous herb delicious with tomatoes and used in all kinds of Italian or Mediterranean-style dishes.

beat   To quickly mix substances.

black pepper   A biting and pungent seasoning, freshly ground pepper is a must for many dishes and adds an extra level of flavor and taste.

blend   To completely mix something, usually with a blender or food processor, more slowly than beating.

blue cheese   A blue-veined cheese that crumbles easily and has a somewhat soft texture, usually sold in a block. The color is from a flavorful, edible mold that is often added or injected into the cheese.

boil   To heat a liquid to a point where water is forced to turn into steam, causing the liquid to bubble. To boil something is to insert it into boiling water. A rapid boil is when a lot of bubbles form on the surface of the liquid.

Brie   A creamy cow's milk cheese from France with a soft, edible rind and a mild flavor.

brown   To cook in a skillet, turning, until the food's surface is seared and brown in color, to lock in the juices.

caramelize   To cook sugar over low heat until it develops a sweet caramel flavor. The term is increasingly gaining use to describe cooking vegetables (especially onions) or meat in butter or oil over low heat until they soften, sweeten, and develop a caramel color.

cayenne   A fiery spice made from (hot) chili peppers, especially the cayenne chili, a slender, red, and very hot pepper.

cheddar   The ubiquitous hard cow's milk cheese with a rich, buttery flavor that ranges from mellow to sharp. Originally produced in England, cheddar is now produced worldwide.

chevre   French for goat's milk cheese, chevre is a typically creamy-salty soft cheese delicious by itself or paired with fruits or chutney. Chevres vary in style from mild and creamy to aged, firm, and flavorful.

chili powder   A seasoning blend that includes chili pepper, cumin, garlic, and oregano. Proportions vary among different versions, but they all offer a warm, rich flavor.

chilis (also **chiles**)   Any one of many different "hot" peppers, ranging in intensity from the relatively mild ancho pepper to the blisteringly hot habañero.

Chinese five-spice powder   A seasoning blend of cinnamon, anise, ginger, fennel, and pepper.

chipotle   Dried jalapeño chilies that have then been smoked. They are canned in a spicy sauce similar to a hot red pepper sauce made from chilies, vinegar, and salt.

chop To cut into pieces, usually qualified by an adverb such as "*coarsely* chopped," or by a size measurement such as "chopped into $\frac{1}{2}$-inch pieces." "Finely chopped" is much closer to mince.

chorizo A spiced pork sausage eaten alone and as a component in many recipes.

chutney A thick condiment often served with Indian curries made with fruits and/or vegetables with vinegar, sugar, and spices.

cilantro A member of the parsley family and used in Mexican cooking and some Asian dishes. Cilantro is what gives some salsas their unique flavor. Use in moderation, as the flavor can overwhelm. The seed of the cilantro is the spice coriander.

cinnamon A sweet, rich, aromatic spice commonly used in baking or desserts. Cinnamon can also be used for delicious and interesting entrées.

clove A sweet, strong, almost wintergreen-flavor spice used in baking and with meats such as ham.

coriander A rich, warm, spicy seed used in all types of recipes, from African to South American, from entrées to desserts.

cornichon The French word for gherkin, and these sweet-tart pickles made from tiny cucumbers are often seen on a plate with patés or smoked meats.

crème fraîche A thickened cream with a tangy flavor similar to sour cream.

crudités Fresh vegetables served as an appetizer, often all together on one tray.

cumin A fiery, smoky-tasting spice popular in Middle-Eastern and Indian dishes. Cumin is a seed; ground cumin seed is the most common form of the spice used in cooking.

curd One of the two products resulting from coagulated milk (the other is whey), curd is a gelatinous substance used to make cheese. Curd also refers to dishes of similar texture, such as dishes make with egg (lemon curd).

custard A cooked mixture of eggs and milk. Custards are a popular base for desserts.

dash A few drops, usually of a liquid, released by a quick shake of, for example, a bottle of hot sauce.

devein The removal of the dark vein from the back of a large shrimp with a sharp knife.

dice To cut into small cubes about ¼-inch square.

Dijon mustard Hearty, spicy mustard made in the style of the Dijon region of France.

dill A unique herb that is perfect for eggs, salmon, cheese dishes, and, of course, vegetables (pickles!).

double boiler A set of two pots designed to nest together, one inside the other. The bottom pot holds water; the top pot holds the ingredient you want to heat.

espresso Strong coffee made by forcing steam through finely ground coffee beans.

fennel In seed form, a fragrant, licorice-tasting herb. The bulbs have a much milder flavor and a celery-like crunch and are used as a vegetable in salads or cooked recipes.

feta This white, crumbly, salty cheese is popular in Greek cooking, on salads, and on its own.

fillet A piece of meat or seafood with the bones removed.

flake To break into thin sections, as with fish.

floret The flower or bud end of broccoli or cauliflower.

garbanzo beans (also **chickpeas**) A yellow-gold, roundish bean that's the base ingredient in hummus.

garlic A member of the onion family, a pungent and flavorful element in many savory dishes.

ginger Available in fresh root, crystallized, or dried, ground form, ginger adds a pungent, sweet, and spicy quality to a dish. It is a very popular element of many Asian and Indian dishes, among others.

Gorgonzola A creamy and rich Italian blue cheese. "Dolce" is sweet, and that's the kind you want.

grappa A clear Italian liqueur distilled from grape skins and grape seeds that is high in alcohol.

grate To shave into tiny pieces using a sharp rasp or grater.

grind To reduce a large, hard substance, often a seasoning such as peppercorns, to the consistency of sand.

Gruyère A rich, sharp cow's milk cheese made in Switzerland. It has a nutty flavor.

Havarti A creamy, Danish, mild cow's milk cheese perhaps most enjoyed in its herbed versions such as Havarti with dill.

herbes de Provence A seasoning mix including basil, fennel, marjoram, rosemary, sage, and thyme, common in the south of France.

hoisin sauce A sweet Asian condiment similar to ketchup made with soybeans, sesame, chili peppers, and sugar.

horseradish A sharp, spicy root that forms the flavor base in many condiments from cocktail sauce to sharp mustards.

infusion A liquid in which flavorful ingredients such as herbs have been soaked or steeped to extract that flavor into the liquid.

Italian breadcrumbs Breadcrumbs seasoned with parsley, other herbs, garlic, and Parmesan cheese.

jicama A juicy, crunchy, sweet, large, round Central American vegetable that is eaten both raw and cooked. If you can't find jicama, try substituting sliced water chestnuts.

kalamata olives Traditionally from Greece, these medium-small long black olives have a smoky rich flavor, very different from run-of-the-mill canned black olives.

kirsch, kirschwasser A clear, tart cherry brandy distilled from cherry juice and cherry pits that lends a characteristic flavor in cheese fondue.

liqueur The general name for a sweet alcoholic beverage made by infusing grain alcohol or a spirit such as rum or brandy with flavoring. The flavoring can be that of fruits, nuts, herbs, or spices.

marinate To soak meat, seafood, or other food in a seasoned sauce, called a marinade, which is high in acid content. The acids break down the muscle of the meat, making it tender and adding flavor.

mascarpone A thick, creamy, spreadable cheese, traditionally from Italy, although versions using the same name are made in the United States.

mince To cut into very small pieces, smaller than diced pieces, about $1/_8$ inch or smaller.

nutmeg A sweet, fragrant, musky spice used primarily in baking.

Old Bay A seasoning mix containing celery salt, mustard, cayenne, bay leaves, cloves, allspice, ginger, and paprika.

olive oil A fragrant liquid produced by crushing or pressing olives. Extra-virgin olive oil is the oil produced from the first pressing of a batch of olives; oil is also produced from other pressings after the first.

olives The fruit of the olive tree commonly grown on all sides of the Mediterranean. There are many varieties of olives but two general types: green and black.

oregano A fragrant, slightly astringent herb used in Greek, Spanish, and Italian dishes.

oyster sauce A thick Asian sauce made from ground oysters, salt, and water with a slightly sweet taste.

panko A Japanese breadcrumb that creates a crunchy crust on baked and fried foods.

paprika A rich, red, warm, earthy spice that also lends a rich red color to many dishes.

Parmesan A hard, dry, flavorful cheese primarily used grated or shredded as a seasoning for Italian-style dishes.

parsley A fresh-tasting green leafy herb used to add color and interest to just about any savory dish.

peppercorns Large, round, dried berries that are ground to produce pepper.

pesto A thick spread or sauce made with fresh basil leaves, garlic, olive oil, pine nuts, and Parmesan cheese. Some newer versions are made with other herbs.

pinch An unscientific measurement term that refers to the amount of an ingredient—typically a dry, granular substance such as an herb or seasoning—you can hold between your finger and thumb.

pita bread A flat, hollow wheat bread that can be used for sandwiches or sliced, pizza style, into slices.

porcini mushrooms Rich and flavorful mushrooms used in rice and Italian-style dishes.

portobello mushrooms A mature and larger form of the smaller crimini mushroom, portobellos are brownish, chewy, and flavorful.

prosciutto Dry, salt-cured ham, that originated in Italy. Prosciutto is popular in many simple dishes in which its unique flavor is allowed to shine.

purée To reduce a food to a thick, creamy texture, usually using a blender or food processor.

raita The generic name given to yogurt-based Indian sauces designed to cool down spicy dishes.

reduce To boil or simmer a broth or sauce to remove some of the water content, resulting in more concentrated flavor and color.

reserve To hold a specified ingredient for another use later in the recipe.

ricotta A fresh Italian cheese smoother than cottage cheese with a slightly sweet flavor.

Roquefort A world-famous (French) creamy but sharp sheep's milk cheese containing blue lines of mold, making it a "blue cheese."

rosemary A pungent, sweet herb used with chicken, pork, fish, and especially lamb. A little of it goes a long way.

roux A mixture of butter or another fat and flour, used to thicken sauces and soups.

sage   An herb with a musty yet fruity, lemon-rind scent and "sunny" flavor. It is a terrific addition to many dishes.

sauté   To pan-cook over lower heat than used for frying.

sesame oil   An oil, made from pressing sesame seeds, that is tasteless if clear and aromatic and flavorful if brown.

shallot   A member of the onion family that grows in a bulb somewhat like garlic and has a milder onion flavor.

shellfish   A broad range of seafood, including clams, mussels, oysters, crabs, shrimp, and lobster. Some people are allergic to shellfish, so care should be taken with its inclusion in recipes.

shiitake mushrooms   Large, dark brown mushrooms originally from the Far East with a hearty, meaty flavor that can be grilled or used as a component in other recipes and as a flavoring source for broth.

shred   To cut into many long, thin slices.

silver skin   The thin, almost iridescent coating on lean cuts of meat like tenderloins that must be trimmed away so the meat doesn't curl when it's cooked.

simmer   To boil gently so the liquid barely bubbles.

skewers   Thin wooden or metal sticks, usually about eight inches long, that are perfect for assembling kebabs, dipping food pieces into fondues, or serving single-bite food items with a bit of panache.

steam   To suspend a food over boiling water and allow the heat of the steam (water vapor) to cook the food. Steaming is a very quick cooking method that preserves the flavor and texture of a food.

Stilton   The famous English blue-veined cheese, delicious with toasted nuts and renowned for its pairing with Port wine.

stock   A flavorful broth made by cooking meats and/or vegetables with seasonings until the liquid absorbs these flavors. This liquid is then strained and the solids discarded.

tahini   A paste made from sesame seeds that is used to flavor many Middle Eastern recipes, especially baba ghanoush and hummus.

tarragon A sweet, rich-smelling herb perfect with seafood, vegetables (especially asparagus), chicken, and pork.

thyme A minty, zesty herb whose leaves are used in a wide range of recipes.

toffee A candy, similar to caramel, made by cooking sugar with water and usually butter until it's browned.

tofu A cheeselike substance made from soybeans and soy milk. Flavorful and nutritious, tofu is an important component of foods across the globe, especially from East Asia.

tomatillo A small, round green tomato with a distinctive spicy flavor. Tomatillos are a traditional component of many south-of-the-border dishes. To use, remove the papery outer skin, rinse off any sticky residue, and chop like a tomato.

turmeric A spicy, pungent yellow root used in many dishes, especially Indian cuisine, for color and flavor. Turmeric is the source of the brilliant yellow color in many prepared mustards.

vinegar An acidic liquid widely used as dressing and seasoning. Many cuisines use vinegars made from different source materials such as fermented grapes, apples, and rice.

walnuts Grown worldwide, walnuts bring a rich, slightly woody flavor to all types of food. For the quick cook, walnuts are available chopped and ready to go at your grocery store. They are delicious toasted and make fine accompaniments to cheeses.

whisk To rapidly mix, introducing air to the mixture.

Worcestershire sauce Originally developed in India and containing tamarind, this spicy sauce is used as a seasoning for many meats and other dishes.

zest Small slivers of peel, usually from a citrus fruit such as lemon, lime, or orange.

Metric Conversion Charts

The scientifically precise calculations needed for baking are not necessary when cooking conventionally or in a slow cooker. The charts in this chapter are designed for general cooking. If you're making conversions for baking, grab your calculator and compute the exact figure.

Converting Ounces to Grams

The numbers in the following table are approximate. To reach the exact number of grams, multiply the number of ounces by 28.35.

Ounces	Grams
1 oz.	30 g
2 oz.	60 g
3 oz.	85 g
4 oz.	115 g
5 oz.	140 g
6 oz.	180 g
7 oz.	200 g
8 oz.	225 g
9 oz.	250 g
10 oz.	285 g
11 oz.	300 g
12 oz.	340 g
13 oz.	370 g
14 oz.	400 g
15 oz.	425 g
16 oz.	450 g

Converting Quarts to Liters

The numbers in the following table are approximate. To reach the exact amount in liters, multiply the number of quarts by 0.95.

Quarts	Liters
1 cup ($\frac{1}{4}$ qt.)	$\frac{1}{4}$ L
1 pt. ($\frac{1}{2}$ qt.)	$\frac{1}{2}$ L
1 qt.	1 L
2 qt.	2 L

Quarts	Liters
2½ qt.	2½ L
3 qt.	2¾ L
4 qt.	3¾ L
5 qt.	4¾ L
6 qt.	5½ L
7 qt.	6½ L
8 qt.	7½ L

Converting Pounds to Grams and Kilograms

The numbers in the following table are approximate. To reach the exact number of grams, multiply the number of pounds by 453.6.

Pounds	Grams; Kilograms
1 lb.	450 g
1½ lb.	675 g
2 lb.	900 g
2½ lb.	1,125 g; 1¼ kg
3 lb.	1,350 g
3½ lb.	1,500 g; 1½ kg
4 lb.	1,800 g
4½ lb.	2kg
5 lb.	2¼ kg
5½ lb.	2½ kg
6 lb.	2¾ kg
6½ lb.	3 kg
7 lb.	3¼ kg
7½ lb.	3½ kg
8 lb.	3¾ kg

Index

D

T

U-V

W

X-Y-Z

Check Out These
Best-Sellers

Grammar and Style
SECOND EDITION

1-59257-115-8
$16.95

Buying and Selling a Home
FOURTH EDITION

1-59257-120-4
$18.95

Being a Groom
SECOND EDITION

0-02-864456-5
$9.95

Learning Spanish
THIRD EDITION

0-02-864451-4
$18.95

Personal Finance in Your 20s & 30s
SECOND EDITION

0-02-864374-7
$19.95

Organizing Your Life
FOURTH EDITION

1-59257-413-0
$16.95

Total Nutrition
FOURTH EDITION

1-59257-439-4
$18.95

Positive Dog Training

0-02-864463-8
$14.95

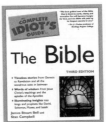

The Bible
THIRD EDITION

1-59257-389-4
$18.95

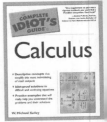

Calculus

0-02-864365-8
$18.95

Music Theory
SECOND EDITION

1-59257-437-8
$19.95

The Perfect Resume
THIRD EDITION

0-02-864440-9
$14.95

Playing the Guitar
SECOND EDITION

0-02-864244-9
$21.95

1-59257-335-5
$19.95

Knitting and Crocheting
SECOND EDITION
Illustrated

1-59257-089-5
$16.95

More than *450 titles* available at booksellers and online retailers everywhere